THIS IS:
ESSAYS ON JAZZ

AARON GILBREATH

Outpost19 | San Francisco
outpost19.com

Gilbreath, Aaron
        This Is: Essays on Jazz / Aaron Gilbreath
        ISBN 9781944853327 (pbk)

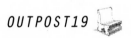

OUTPOST19

ORIGINAL
PROVOCATIVE
READING

Also by
Aaron Gilbreath

Everything We Don't Know

This book is for you Dad, secret pianist, for introducing me to not just jazz, but music itself, and showing me how good it feels to swing. It's Satchmo, Duke and you, Dad, now and always.

THIS IS:
ESSAYS ON JAZZ

Contents

Introduction

If Frank Zappa or Elvis Costello, or whoever originally said it, was correct that "writing about music is like dancing about architecture," then why has music led to so much powerful writing? Jazz in particular has proven rich literary material. Geoff Dyer's book *But Beautiful*, Michael Ondaatje's 1976 novel *Coming Through Slaughter*, John Clellon Holmes's 1958 novel *The Horn*, James D. Houston's novel *Gig*, Luc Sante's haunting *Believer* essay "I Thought I Heard Buddy Bolden Say," not to mention countless articles, poems, fiction and essays by Ellen Willis, David Gates, Yusef Komunyaaka and Langston Hughes, all stemming directly from music.

Jazz guitarist Kenny Burrell appears in Ryu Murakami's 1997 novel *In the Miso Soup*. Louis Armstrong features as a central character in Roddy Doyle's novel *Oh, Play That Thing*. The popular anime series *Cowboy Bebop* takes part of its name from jazz's pioneering mid-century form. Haruki Murakami features photographer Hozumi Nakadaira's popular jazz coffee shop New Dug in his novel *Norwegian Wood*, and Murakami mentions pianist Tommy Flanagan in his story "Chance Traveler." Dancing about architecture? Not always. Music is the eternal well-spring. My favorite music writing doesn't critique the music or limit itself to describing how it sounds. It preoccupies itself with the writer's reaction to the music—how the sound makes the writer think or feel, or what it means to them—as well as how the music fits into the larger scope of history, what it reveals about interpersonal relationships and the broader culture. I also love stories about the musicians themselves, their lives and humanity. Music isn't a thing, some abstraction separate from the human condition. It *is* the human condition, and I, as a reader, writer and listener, live for the narratives of achievement, heartbreak, success, failure, struggle, disappearance, cult status, determination, emotion and innovation, music's lifeblood and our shared existence. From the enduring fire of Loretta Lynn to the strange fierce fizzle of Bix Beiderbecke, when it comes to this kind of music writing, you could write about music forever and not once dance about architecture. At least, that's the kind of music writing that moves me. Hopefully there's a little of that in the essays I've collected here. As Charlie Parker said, "They teach you there's a boundary line to music. But, man, there's no boundary line to art." May jazz and writing forever mingle.

Jimmy Smith and
the Allure of the Vault

Imagine a completely different version of one one of jazz's most revered compositions sitting on a shelf in a Los Angeles office building for three decades without anyone knowing it. When twenty-seven year old jazz enthusiast Michael Cuscuna finally gained access to the Blue Note Records vault in 1975, he not only found an alternate take of Thelonious Monk's "Well You Needn't," but scores of unissued, album-length recordings. On his first day inside, Cuscuna stood amid rows of Scotch 3M master tapes and told the man who brought him, "This is great." He'd been hounding another Blue Note executive for three years to gain access, enticing him with offers to catalog and identify the vault's voluminous contents. Ever since musicians in New York started telling Cuscuna stories about the sessions they had played on but never seen released, he'd grown obsessed with this undiscovered music and started recording details in a notebook. Now, here he was, surrounded by the lost recordings of legendary guitarist Grant Green, saxophonist Hank Mobley, trumpeters Lee Morgan and Blue Mitchell, and drummer Art Blakey—brilliant players who defined post-Bop jazz in the 1950s and '60s and helped make Blue Note jazz's most important label. "The experience was staggering," Cuscuna said. "There were far more unissued sessions than I had even imagined." Many of those sessions belonged to organist Jimmy Smith.

In the annals of music history, Smith will forever be known as the person who transformed the Hammond B-3 organ from a chirpy, ice skating rink novelty into an expressive instrument. With his driving, bluesy style, Smith solidified the organ trio format in the jazz tradition and led the way from Be Bop to Soul Jazz. Lest you imagine organ music as dentist office easy listening, know this: when Smith first started performing in New York in 1956, jazz was acoustic. Although horns were often played in clubs near a central, ambient microphone, guitars were generally the only instrument that required electricity to produce their sound, and even then they were run through amplifiers free of effects, employing only their natural, open tone. When Smith plugged in his B-3, the sounds he produced were as groundbreaking stylistically as The Ramones's two-minute punk songs or surf guitarist Dick Dale playing Eastern scales through a Fender Reverb unit in 1961. No wonder Miles Davis described Smith as "the eighth wonder of the world."

As a diehard Jimmy Smith fan, I was thrilled last year to discover that, in the late 1990s and early 2000s, Cuscuna released four of the Smith recordings he found in the vault.

I owned the organist's entire Blue Note and early-Verve catalog, many of the albums so infectious that each playing left me in a nearly drug-addled froth craving more. Yet, despite my years of fandom, two of the new albums had somehow eluded my notice. *Cherokee* and *Lonesome Road* were both released in 1996 exclusively in Japan, a country that, for its size, boasts an unusually large, dedicated jazz audience. Limited releases hadn't slowed my purchasing habits before. I bought a number of expensive Japanese imports online: organist Freddie Roach's *Down to Earth*, trombonist Curtis Fuller's *Volume 3*. Even though our digital age offers instant acquisition through file-sharing sites, high prices and long distances were no barrier to acquiring the physical album and its superior fidelity. What worried me was listenability. Were these albums as good as Smith's best from the period, such as *Home Cookin'*, *Crazy! Baby* and *Midnight Special?* Or had they been in the vault for a reason? I'd run into problems before.

When I bought Hank Mobley's elusive *Poppin'*, I was disappointed. Recorded in 1957, the album features some of jazz's best players—pianist Sonny Clark, drummer Philly Joe Jones—and sat in the vault for twenty-three years before Cuscuna released it in Japan. My hands nearly trembled when I first opened that rare CD's jewel case. It proved unremarkable. Only two songs were stirring, and one, "Darn That Dream," was a popular cover available on countless jazz albums. In the parlance of record reviewers,

Poppin' was a standard Hard bop date composed of predictable compositions neither abysmal nor memorable. The same happened with trumpeter Dizzy Reece's *Comin' On!*. Recorded in 1960, locked away for thirty-nine years, I bought the CD, played it, then shoved it on a shelf as if it had never left the vault.

Which isn't to say that Cuscuna's discoveries were all lackluster—quite the opposite. His determination and meticulous archival work liberated numerous masterpieces from the metaphorical tyranny of the corporate vault and, in the process, filled gaps in music history and doubled jazz fans' record collections. All of saxophonist Tina Brooks' posthumous releases; Grant Green's *Matador*; vibraphonist Bobby Hutcherson's first session, *The Kicker*; Lee Morgan's *The Procrastinator*; Mobley's *Another Workout*—each on par with the leaders' most celebrated albums. Had it been his only discovery, Andrew Hill's adventurous nonet, *Passing Ships*, would confirm the importance of Cuscuna's efforts, but he also discovered the rest of Sonny Rollins' searing live set from *A Night at the Village Vanguard*, not to mention that Monk tune. But my experience with Smith's recently unearthed music had established two distinct poles between which everything thereafter would fall.

Two of them, *Six Views of the Blues* and *Straight Life*, came out in the US as limited editions, and I owned them. Smith's cover of W.C. Handy's "St. Louis Blues" on *Six View* burns with the deep, in the pocket groove Smith is celebrated for, and his melodic originals "Blues No. 1" and "Blues No. 2" are rousing enough to fit easily on *Home Cookin'* or *Midnight Special*. This only makes the songs' forty-one year dormancy more beguiling. Not so with the other album.

Straight Life, a session from 1961, includes a few moving originals, such as "Jimmy's Blues" and the title track, but even as the album's standouts, each resemble repeats of tunes on his other records. The rest feel like filler—how many covers of "Star Dust" and "Yes Sir, That's My Baby" do listeners need?—forming a program so nondescript as to place it in that dreaded record collector graveyard known as "nonessential listening." I could understand why Blue Note co-founders Alfred Lion and Francis Wolff shelved *Straight Life* in favor of Smith's more memorable sessions. Yet it's the curse of the fan to always crave more music, and because the allure of the vault exerts such a strong psychic hold, I did what most obsessive fans do upon learning of new releases: I trolled the web for prices and shipping options.

To those for whom music is more than some casual, tertiary interest, the very idea of the record company vault possesses a mythic, Ark of the Covenant quality. Less in jazz than rock and roll, the locked and restricted storage spaces known as "vaults," and their famously unreleased contents, are part of the mythology. *Smile* by The Beach Boys; Boy Dylan's 1966 Royal Albert Hall concert; The

Beatles' pre-Phil Spector mix of *Let It Be*, entitled *Get Back*; the infamous "Million Dollar Quartet" jam session featuring Elvis, Jerry Lee Lewis, Johnny Cash and Carl Perkins, recorded at Sun Studios in 1956—all of these masterworks sat in vaults for decades, simultaneously tantalizing and tormenting fans while accruing more iconic weight than their contents seemed able to bear. Then the bands released them, and the wait proved worthwhile: the music was brilliant. Dylan released the Royal Albert Hall show in 1998 as part of his official Bootleg Series. The Beatles released an approximation of *Let It Be*'s original, thirty-four year old mix as *Let It Be... Naked* in 2003. "The Million Dollar Quartet" emerged in various official forms in the 1980s, 1990s and 2006. And when The Beach Boys finally put out *Smile* in 2011 as *The Smile Sessions*, they ended its reign as the world's most famous unreleased album, a debut forty-four years in the making. Before the artists sanctioned these releases, though, the music circulated among fans on bootlegs.

Coined during Prohibition when people smuggled hooch in tall boots, the term bootleg now mainly refers to unauthorized albums pressed without record company sanction and sold to fans without profiting the copyright holder. When the music isn't live material recorded by a concertgoer with a microphone, it's usually something unearthed through the furtive methods of a tomb raider: namely, someone pillages a collection of source tapes, either from a company vault or a musician's private stash.

In 2007, Led Zeppelin guitarist Jimmy Page went to court in Glasgow, Scotland to testify against a bootlegger named Robert Langley. Langley faced twelve counts of selling copyrighted Zeppelin, Yardbirds and Page solo material without authorization. Unlike the usual live audience recordings, Langley's stock drew from tapes that had been stolen from Page's home in the early 1980s. Among the many multi-track soundboard concert recordings that were snatched from Page's huge personal archive, there were also Zeppelin rehearsal tapes, studio outtakes and concert footage. In the years after the break-in, the Zeppelin bootleg market swelled with previously uncirculated audio and video, and bootleggers did what they'd done since the first rock bootleg, the Bob Dylan LP *Great White Wonder*, appeared on West Coast record stores shelves in 1969: they bootlegged the bootlegs to rerelease the material. In the process, sound quality deteriorated, but the music reached an increasingly wide audience, which satisfied listeners despite the fidelity.

Page had no problem with fans trading live recordings with each other; in court, he described the practice as "legitimate." What he objected to were illicit commercial enterprises overcharging fans for what were often subpar live recordings that sounded, in his words, like "just a whirring" where "you cannot hear the music." Langley's bootlegs belonged to a higher class. In court, Page told a story about how he'd once gone into a large Manhattan record store to, in his words, "check what they had for the band and Jimmy Page," and discovered a live album recorded in 1975 at London's Earl's Court. "I do not know where it surfaced from," he said, "but I contacted my New York lawyers to say the shop was selling something as if it was official, but clearly it was not." The album's sound and packaging were of such high quality that the store assumed it was a sanctioned release. The shop removed it, but there was no stopping the underground trade. Like Langley's, it was one among thousands. Hearing stories like these, you can't help but wonder what other treasures lurk in the world's unplundered vaults.

On that first day in the vault, Cuscuna cut the cord that bound together six reels from an early-60s Jackie McLean session, and when he opened the box, there were no papers inside. He looked at other reels. None of them had papers. No song titles, no sidemen's names or composer credits, just the name of the session leader written on the box, along with the recording date and reel number. Frustrated, Cuscuna walked to the studio and asked, "So where's all the paperwork for this stuff?" "There is none," everyone said. The files had gone missing since a larger company bought and moved Blue Note from New York to LA. So began what Cuscuna called the greatest and worst day of his life. "My dream had come true," he said, "and now it was my worst nightmare."

To identify the contents, Cuscuna would listen to the music, try to identify the players by their stylistic signatures, and then study musicians' union contracts and check what songs Blue Note's publishing company copyrighted within weeks of each recording. This gave him song titles and sidemen's names. In the 1970s and '80s, many Blue Note musicians were still alive and performing, so Cuscuna would send them tapes and ask for information.

It took a few years, but as his detective work yielded results, Cuscuna began releasing the material. Fans were thrilled. After he'd issued about twenty albums, someone at King Records, the label which licensed Blue Note music in Japan, mailed him a Xerox of a document that Alfred Lion had made, listing most of the unissued sessions' details, along with comments. That, Cuscuna said, "would've made my life a lot easier early on."

Somewhere in Japan sat my two Jimmy Smith albums. I read peoples' impressions on various websites. I studied the session information. I pictured the CDs sitting in a distributor's cavernous warehouse, waiting for me to call them out from among the crates of CDs and LPs. I never ordered them.

As much as I wanted to hear the music, I also liked knowing there was more out there to be discovered. The notion is comforting, tied up with the kind of excitement and awe that you feel as a child when gazing over a fence at an expanse of undeveloped desert or a patch of neighborhood woods. "What's out there?" you wonder, anticipation tightening your chest. Even if you never venture into it, the idea that such a wild tangle exists reminds you of the universe's essential mystery. In our era where everything has been photographed from space and is searchable from your portable communication device, vaults are the world before 1412, the unexplored corners during the Age of Discovery. They're the coelacanth captured in a fisherman's net. The new planet discovered six hundred light-years away.

Maybe I'm being romantic, or maybe fainthearted, but I'd rather live with the enigmatic charm of these albums' distant existence than bear the potential disappointment of their shortcomings. When an artist dies, they often leave a backlog of material both finished and unfinished, and at some point fans must accept that what we have has to be enough, that we've reached the end of the oeuvre. Readers have experienced this in literature. Ernest Hemingway's posthumous novel, *True at First Light*, was finished by his second son Patrick, published thirty-eight years after its author's suicide, and widely regarded as a disappointing bookend to Hemingway's creative life. More recently, an editor at publisher Little, Brown and Company shaped David Foster Wallace's final novel, *The Pale King*, into its published form from drafts, fragments and notes, leaving us a memorable, challenging work that doesn't try to hide its incompleteness. *The Pale King* offers strong evidence that there is value in publishing certain unfinished material, while *True at First Light* suggests that in other cases it's best to stop before reaching the bottom of the proverbial barrel. Sometimes the bottom contains the strongest, most concentrated flavors; other times it contains the dregs. I didn't want to go there with Jimmy Smith.

Rather than the inferior artifact, I choose to live with mystery's invigorating companionship, with the notion that maybe, just maybe, there is something else waiting in that vault, something as bluesy and red hot as "Alfredo" on *Crazy! Baby*, music so monumental that it makes you wonder how it could hide in plain sight for so long, right under our noses, without anybody noticing.

Don't Worry 'Bout Me:
The Brief Career and
Self-Imposed Exile of Jutta Hipp

On July 28, 1956, German jazz pianist Jutta Hipp and American saxophonist Zoot Sims recorded eight songs in Rudy Van Gelder's home studio in Hackensack, New Jersey. Back in her native country, Hipp's swinging, percussive style had earned her the title of Europe's first lady of jazz, and she took the moniker with her when she moved to New York City in 1955. On the recommendation of critic and composer Leonard Feather, the venerable Blue Note Records signed her, making her the label's first white female and European instrumentalist on a roster composed largely of American men of color. In 1956, Blue Note recorded her live at the Hickory House, a beloved venue and steakhouse in Midtown Manhattan, where she did a six-month residency. Blue Note released the performance as a two-record set. *Jutta Hipp with Zoot Sims* was her first studio album in America. Sims's rich tone and easy air paired well with Hipp's rollicking, energetic playing, and the album they created together is arguably her finest.

Hipp played clubs around New York. She toured. In

1956, she performed at the famous Newport Jazz Festival on a bill that included Count Basie, Charles Mingus and the Modern Jazz Quartet. Newport was the ideal venue for a musician seeking a wider audience, which was precisely what Leonard Feather sought for Hipp when he encouraged her to move to the United States in the first place, and it was why he helped her secure a visa, why he and his wife put her up for a few months on the top floor of their home, why he brought her to Blue Note, introduced her to booking agent Joe Glaser, helped sort things out with the local musicians' union, and initially functioned as her cultural liaison, her advocate and essentially her agent. Feather had helped other musicians like Dizzy Gillespie and Sarah Vaughn write, record and book gigs. He was a businessman. He made money off music. But money and recognition were more Feather's goals than Hipp's. She didn't even want to lead her own band. In 1960, with six albums to her name, she quit with no explanation. She never performed publically again, and she told so few people about her previous life in music that most of her friends and factory coworkers only discovered it in her obituary. For the next forty-one years, Jutta patched garments for a living, painted, drew, and took photos for pleasure—all while royalties accrued on Blue Note's books.

Hipp's records had never been big sellers in the United States. Her identity was obscure even to ardent jazz fans. But *Jutta Hipp with Zoot Sims* and her three other Blue

Note records sold well in Japan. Japan is a hotbed of jazz fandom. They love Be Bop and Hard bop, and they've long been one of the strongest markets for Blue Note's classic 1950s and '60s sessions. When it comes to jazz there, the more obscure the better. Hipp was that, and it earned her and Blue Note a lot of money. Hipp just wasn't getting any of it. When she quit performing, she severed contact with the label as well as with most of the people who could have told Blue Note where to send her checks.

•

In 2001, Tom Evered, then Blue Note's general manager, did some research on the money the label owed to Hipp and was surprised by what he found. "I think on her own," he said, "Jutta would have just been too shy, or too self-deprecating, to get on the phone and check on royalties." In order to get Hipp what she'd earned and to clear the company's books, Evered got her phone number from Gundula Konitz, the wife of influential saxophonist Lee Konitz. The Konitzes were among the few people she kept in touch with from her jazz days. When he reached Hipp, he told her he had good news: There was around $35,000 dollars in her royalties account, and he wanted to cut her a check.

The line fell silent. Seconds passed. Then, in her heavy German accent, she said, "Mein Gott."

"I just had to laugh," Evered recalled. At that time, Hipp was seventy-six years old, unmarried, living on Social Security and a little union pension, with no family in America. "She couldn't believe it. I mean, to come out of nowhere with that much money."

Most Blue Note artists had been receiving royalty checks through the years. In a big, well-managed label, royalties accrue automatically. But if a musician moved, died or disappeared, and no one notified the company, the checks got returned. Then they were sent a second time, via registered mail, and if they were returned again, the royalty department filed them under what Evered called "the Bad Address list." After discovering Hipp's unclaimed royalties, Evered said, "I kind of became a detective for the company, trying to dig up estates or actually find the people, which was pretty interesting, especially when I called up [tenor saxophonist] Hank Mobley's father to let him know that there were—I can't remember exactly how much, but it might have been eighty-something thousand dollars." Although Mobley had been a regular session musician and staple of the Blue Note catalog, his sales were never big. After he died, in 1986, his family and the company lost touch, and the royalties piled up—until Evered found the family. He did the same with Blossom Dearie.

Popular in the 1950s and '60s, Dearie was a pianist-chanteuse who put out numerous albums on Verve but only one on Capitol Records: the breezy, thirty-minute-long *May I Come In*. Because EMI owned Capitol and Blue Note, Evered called Dearie. "She had this little girly voice, and she said, 'Oh Tom, I don't get any royalty checks anymore.' Even though the record's kind of short and had been in and out of print for a while, it was a few thousand dollars here and there. I said, 'Blossom, did you move?' She said, 'Oh, yeah.'" This happened regularly, but the royalty system placed the onus on the musician to keep in touch with the company, not on the company to track down musicians. "And Jutta," Evered said, "had not gotten any royalties in a *long* time."

Rather than mail Hipp her check, Evered arranged to hand-deliver it. He and Astrid Heppner, secretary to Blue Note president Bruce Lundvall, had a car service drive them from the company's offices to Hipp's apartment in Sunnyside, Queens. As their car sped east, Manhattan's skyline dipped below the jumble of warehouses and apartments that filled this pocket of Queens. Visiting retired musicians was far from the usual sales and marketing jobs Evered performed as general manager. Heppner typically answered the phones and scheduled meetings. Reflecting on the errand, Evered thought it was as if they were bringing Hipp more than money. This was, he said, "money coming from a world she had left a long time ago."

•

Barely seven minutes into Thomas Reichman's documentary *Mingus: Charlie Mingus 1968*, the great bassist mentions Hipp. "A piano player friend of mine, Jutta Hipp, from Germany, was there when, um, she said she saw the beginnings of it—and this was eight years ago she told me, here in New York—the beginning of Hitler's so-called rise." Mingus lowers his head as if watching a fugitive thought, then lifts his gaze up to the camera crew. "She's a great piano player," he says, smiling. "She's better than Toshiko [Akiyoshi], incidentally. You've heard of Jutta Hipp? Yuh-tuh Hi*pp*. Yuttahipp." Off-camera, the filmmaker says, "Yeah, you told me about her."

Though Hipp considered herself an amateur musician, she arrived in the United States in November, 1955 with a solid reputation. Born in Leipzig in 1925, she learned classical piano at age nine from a church organist. She lived in a musical house. "My father played piano," Hipp said in a 1998 interview in Marge Hofacre's defunct magazine *Jazz News*, "my mother sang terribly." By age thirteen, the noise her family made at home drove Hipp nuts, so she started tuning into the radio stations that the Nazis had forbidden. Families kept their lights off at night because of air raids. After her family went to sleep, she sat alone in the dark, listening to jazz stations. "I heard Count Basie and Fats Waller and Jimmie Lunceford," she told one interviewer, "and I wrote down some of the tunes with a little light there." She also heard jazz at the popular Leipzig Hot Club.

A local drummer owned tons of jazz records, from Duke Ellington to Belgian bands, items that were hard to obtain in Nazi Germany. Using her piano skills to figure out this new music, Hipp jammed with other jazz musicians at the club, before and during the war. When Soviet troops took control of Leipzig in 1946, she fled west to the Allied-occupied zones.

She crossed the border at Tegernsee in the Alps. "There was a group of us," she said in 1998. "We found out by word of mouth where they had the crossing. We had some money with us and some liquor, and we had to give it to the guide. Some woman was too loud, and he told her to stay back. We tried to cross at one place but there were guards there. So we went to another place. At a certain time, we walked down the hill and across the dirt road in the country. And then we were in West Germany. The guide said that when we saw the barracks, we would be in West Germany. Then we went into the barracks, and there were others in there who had crossed. Oh, it was scary." The drummer with the jazz records crossed with her group, as did a professor from the Leipzig Academy of Art, where Hipp had studied visual art as a teenager. She brought her records, some photos, paintings and books. The only clothes she had were the ones she was wearing. Her first change of clothing in her new home was a dress made out of an army blanket.

In West Germany, she played in a circus band. She

played in nightclubs for civilians and in military clubs for American soldiers. In Munich, she played at a venue called the Bongo Bar. "The place was full of little huts and leopards and monkeys," she said, "and the customers sat on small bongo drums instead of on chairs. The leopards were supposed to be tame, but I was always scared to death of them." Life was better, but tough. "We had to play from, say, seven to five in the morning with one break," she said. "Sometimes we played seven days a week, and sometimes we played in the afternoon too. That was murder. You just worked, slept, ate, worked, slept, ate. That's all you did." After playing in other people's bands throughout the late 1940s and early 1950s, she formed her own quintet in 1953, and recorded three albums as a leader for German labels. That same year, she toured Germany with Dizzy Gillespie.

Initially enthralled by the swing pianists she'd heard in Leipzig, her range later expanded when she discovered bop innovator Bud Powell and the bluesy, hard-driving Horace Silver. Her style wowed listeners. Not only that, but her gender: here was a woman leading her own band. Jazz was a predominately male world, and still is, with women working almost exclusively as vocalists. Hipp, however, didn't set out to blaze trails. She was playing piano because she enjoyed it. But Hipp was aware of the lure and marketability of her gender. As she told one interviewer, if she was well known in Germany, it was "Because I was female, I guess." Later, this reputation would put immense pressure on her, but it also helped launch her U.S. career.

In 1948, she gave birth to a son who she named Lionel, after one of her favorite vibraphonists, Lionel Hampton. The father was a US soldier stationed in Germany. He was African-American. The segregated military didn't allow GIs of color to claim paternity with white women. The GI returned home, his identity unclear, and Hipp gave Lionel up for adoption.

Around 1950 or '51, an American soldier in Munich recorded Hipp's band and mailed a copy to Leonard Feather. Feather was a big name. Jazz artists like Duke Ellington, Louis Jordan, Dinah Washington and Count Basie performed his compositions. He'd penned album liner notes, produced records and written for publications such as *Down Beat*. The tape proved pivotal. While touring Germany with Billie Holiday in 1954, Feather caught Hipp performing in a club in Duisburg and was knocked out by both her playing and, it seems, her beauty. Hipp had long black hair. Her eyes seemed permanently set at half-mast, making her look sultry. Her powerful piano style only multiplied her charms.

In his memoir *The Jazz Years*, Feather says that after their meeting, he "corresponded with her for several months, [and] she began to express interest in coming to America." As she said, "[T]he real good musicians were in America." The immigration paperwork took a while, as did her decision to move. Was it wise to leave Germany?

How would she survive in America, as a single, non-native English speaker? But what reason did she have to stay? After WWII, her country lay in ruins. Her taxing nightclub engagements never earned her much money. After what Feather called "a long period of indecision," Hipp boarded a passenger ship to New York. When she arrived, in 1955, Feather met her at the pier.

Using his connections and Hipp's reputation, Feather laid the groundwork for what he hoped would be an auspicious start to a long career. He talked to New York City club owners and promoters to get her gigs. He convinced Blue Note's co-founders Alfred Lion and Francis Wolff, both German immigrants, to issue one of her German albums in the U.S., retitled *New Faces—New Sounds from Germany*. When the house pianist at the Hickory House went on tour, Feather got Hipp a six-month headlining stint there. It looked like her career might proceed as Feather envisioned. But that didn't happen.

Hipp was shy. Although she loved playing music, she preferred performing for fun rather than for a living, and even then, only to small audiences. Large venues terrified her. Performance anxiety was already an issue during her first months in New York. The day after her debut at the Hickory House in 1956, *New Yorker* writer Whitney Balliett reported that Hipp "was still recovering from the stagefright she'd suffered the night before." "I'm *so* glad to be here," Hipp told Balliett, "and *so* anxious to succeed."

•

In the early and mid-1950s, New York was the crucible of jazz. The music originated in New Orleans, but it rapidly evolved and diversified in New York. Everyone from Miles Davis to Art Blakey regularly played in the clubs, and pianists like Monk, Wynton Kelly and Kelly Drew were recording as sidemen. "You go from playing jazz in a small German club that's maybe the only jazz club within fifty miles," Evered said, "to playing 52nd Street, or playing around the Village, when Thelonious Monk might drop by to see what you're up to, or Bud Powell might come in." That's a lot of pressure. Hipp recalled Duke Ellington coming into the Hickory House every night to eat steak. "I saw him a lot," she said.

Hipp arrived in New York at the end of the bop era. Charlie Parker, one of its architects, had died nine months earlier. Popular as it was, bop seemed increasingly trapped in its own conventions. The speedy chord changes and patterns that had once separated it from swing were now familiar, even restrictive, and musicians were searching for new modes of expression. Blue Note players like Horace Silver and Art Blakey reacted with a new bluesy, gospel-infused form called Hard bop. Miles Davis and John Coltrane reacted in distinctive ways, too, Davis with experiments in "cool jazz" as well as by structuring songs and solos on modal scales instead of chord progressions, and Coltrane by playing unique chord progressions in a style that became known as his "sheets of sound." Jutta floated somewhere between tradition and innovation, a fan of Silver's thunderous, rhythmic approach but not an architect of the new. She played what she liked to listen to without feeling compelled to overthrow the old order. The album *Jutta Hipp with Zoot Sims* exemplifies this. Sims, like Hipp, was a straight-ahead player: not experimental, not pushing stylistic boundaries, but rather approachable, swinging, compellingly listenable. That captures the tone of their collaboration—mostly standards, done straight but well. That might also be their legacy, as practitioners but not trendsetters, loveable but not radical. Still, her reputation and talent—as well as Feather's endorsement— set her apart, so when Blue Note offered her a contract, she signed it.

Through the record company, she became peers with some of jazz's biggest names: Miles Davis, Horace Silver, Sonny Rollins, Thelonious Monk. She also became the label's first white female and European instrumentalist. This wasn't an exception to some label bias. It was a reflection of the talent pool from which Blue Note pulled. Wolff and Lion didn't need to look far beyond New York City to find musicians, and most of them happened to be American men of color. Blue Note did sign Serge Chaloff and Gil Mellé, both white. And there were plenty of talented players in cities like Detroit, Philadelphia and St.

Louis. But many of them moved to New York to work, and even more went under-recorded and were, in turn, lost to history. Though female jazz instrumentalists like Jutta existed, compared to female singers like Billie Holiday and Ella Fitzgerald, they were scarce.

There was pianist Beryl Booker, who taught herself to play, never learned how to read music, led her own all-female trio in the '50s, and opened for Billie Holiday in Germany every night on her 1954 tour. There was pianist Barbara Carroll from Massachusetts, who earned raves from *Down Beat* and played for decades. There was the Japanese pianist that Mingus mentioned, Toshiko Akiyoshi, who moved to the United States in 1956 after her talent caught the attention of record-label owner Norman Granz and pianist Oscar Peterson. The pianist whom Hipp temporarily replaced at the Hickory House was a woman named Marian McPartland. And then there was the precursor to them all, Mary Lou Williams, a versatile, respected pianist raised in Kansas City, who worked with everyone from Louis Armstrong to Benny Goodman and played until age seventy-one. But few of these women were taken as seriously as their male counterparts, and they had to constantly prove themselves. As Beryl Booker said, "They didn't want no woman playing no piano. So I had to say, move off the bench, daddy-o, here I am."

During 1956, Hipp and Feather parted ways. The split was not amicable. He had suggested she record some of his compositions. She declined. Popular jazz and blues singer Dinah Washington had recorded a few of Feather's songs and had success with them. Etta James and Billie Holiday had, too. In 1951, Louis Jordan recorded Feather's "How Blue Can You Get," and when B.B. King recorded the song in 1964, he had such a huge hit with it that it became a standard part of his repertoire. Jutta didn't work that way. She preferred recording songs that she was drawn to naturally—not suggestions, not possible hits or crowd-pleasers, but songs she liked on their own merits.

Hipp not only turned down his compositions, she turned down his advances. Although Feather's memoir makes no mention of any sexual tension or personal conflict, Hipp's biographer Katja von Schuttenbach interviewed musicians who knew Hipp and said that Feather pursued Hipp romantically once she was in the United States. Feather was married and a father at the time, and Jutta was engaged, though only briefly, to a Hungarian guitarist named Atilla Zoller. She'd played with Zoller back in Germany. Even though they called off their engagement after he moved to the United States in 1956, Zoller and Hipp remained lifelong friends.

Von Schuttenbach has been researching Hipp since 2005 as part of her master's thesis, and she intends to publish a biography, which will contain a full account of Feather's role in Hipp's life. Part of this account will include the way Feather retaliated, turning Hipp, in von

Schuttenbach's words, "from protégée to persona non grata." As evidence, von Schuttenbach cites the complete absence of concert reviews or published press material for any of Hipp's six months at the Hickory House. (Feather had written about Hipp four times in the German magazine *Jazz-Echo*, but the last piece appeared in January, 1957.) She also cites Feather's disparaging descriptions of Hipp in both his memoir and his canonical work, *The Encyclopedia of Jazz.*

In his memoir, Feather writes that Hipp's playing changed for the worse in the United States, when she "came under the influence of Horace Silver." This, he believed, "seemed to have the effect of destroying Jutta's individuality." Feather characterizes her retirement as a "loss to jazz of a potentially significant talent," but he blames her for it. "Her personality was a major problem," he says. "Extraordinarily withdrawn and totally without self-confidence, she was very near-sighted but refused to wear glasses." And yet, one wants to say, she did headline gigs like the Hickory House and Newport, and she was assured enough to make numerous records.

Hipp was also a talented visual artist, which Feather mentions only to disparage. "Much of her spare time in New York," he writes, "was spent doing black-and-white sketches in a style I found somewhat frightening, all the faces, even those of friends we knew to be cheerful and perhaps handsome people, somehow looked gross, menacing and ugly." A few of Hipp's drawings have appeared in print. Some of the players have bulging eyes. Some have deep facial lines, protruding lips and dark shading around the eyes. They're hardly frightening. Curiously, Feather never mentions their falling out. He never hints that professional disagreements, or the nature of the music business, might have played a part in her retirement. He only says, "By 1958 we had lost touch with her; word reached us that she had taken a day job at a tailor's shop."

The first edition of Feather's *The Encyclopedia of Jazz*, published in 1955, included an entry about Hipp. By 1966, Feather had removed her entry, commenting in the preface that she was no longer "a conspicuously active figure on today's jazz scene."

In 1958, Hipp failed to pay the rent on her apartment, in Manhattan, and had to move. She took a room for two weeks at the Alvin Hotel, a now-demolished building on 52nd Street where many musicians lived, including Lester Young, Curtis Fuller, and Yusef Lateef. "I saw him in his room," Hipp said of Lester Young. "He had a tiny room with a bed in the middle and no window. And on the sides of the bed were all kinds of bums sleeping. And when he came downstairs, he was all dressed up smiling and waiting…. The Alvin Hotel was terrible." After the Alvin, she moved into another hotel, and finally into an apartment on Horatio Street in the Village. When she got a job at the garment factory in Queens, she found an apartment nearby.

Regardless of the story Feather tells about Hipp, she did begin in 1958, to perform less often. She worked at the factory during the week, and she performed on weekends and on her days off. Instead of Manhattan, she kept to smaller venues, like the Continental Club in Bedford-Stuyvesant, and Copa City in Jamaica, Queens. She loved these clubs. The venues were intimate. The audiences were enthusiastic and the owners nice. Innumerable musicians hung out and played in them, so Hipp met everyone from Coltrane to James Moody to Fats Waller's son Maurice. According to letters that von Schuttenbach has obtained, Hipp's fondness for these clubs reflected her belief that jazz was an intimate art form best experienced in small venues. In the late 1950s, she toured the American South with saxophonist Jesse Powell's band. It was a scrappy tour that generated little money, but Hipp enjoyed it so much she counted it as one of the high points of her career. In a1998 interview, Hipp said, "I want people to know that the real jazz happens in the little clubs." She also said: "I don't go to those places [where the well-known musicians play]. I go to those little unknown places, where the musicians love to play. There's nothing arranged there, you know. They just play and enjoy it. All these other places have arranged music, and [the musicians] always play it the same way. And [the public doesn't] like it unless they do it the same way."

By 1960, however, Hipp had quit music altogether. The

Continental Club closed, and gigs dried up. Copa City's owner, Murray Jupiter, closed his club in frustration. "On the last night, he couldn't take it anymore," Hipp said. "He took all the glasses he had behind the bar, and he smashed everything." Without her favorite haunts, she relied on the factory. "It saved my life," she said. "Because I couldn't survive any other way."

Without piano in her life, Hipp spent her time painting and drawing. She was hardly the only prominent jazz musician to quit. Trumpeter Jabbo Smith played like the Dizzy Gillespie of his era, "as good as Louis [Armstrong in 1930]," according to bassist Milt Hinton, but by the late 1950s, he'd taken a job at Avis Rent a Car in Milwaukee. Composer-saxophonist Gigi Gryce, who wrote some memorable jazz standards, quit performing and became a teacher. The financial and emotional strains of a career in music overwhelmed him. His second-to-last album is called *The Rat Race Blues*.

Hipp's factory job was a union gig working for the once thriving Wallachs men's clothing chain. "I just stayed there because it was easy," she said. "It didn't take much out of me, you know. I still had enough time to paint.... I really didn't care what they made if the people were nice."

Meanwhile, American music continued to change. Free jazz developed out of more melodic, rhythmic forms like Hard bop and went so far out that it no longer resembled the music Hipp had played. At the same time, rock and roll eclipsed jazz as the people's music, pushing Blue Note and its players into the cultural margins, and sending record sales plummeting. The label's owner transferred the offices and master tapes from Manhattan to Los Angeles. There, far from the East Coast urban environment that created the music, its legacy sat neglected, until younger generations rediscovered mid-century jazz during the 1980s, and a visionary producer and fan named Michael Cuscuna spearheaded a program of reissues and previously unheard releases. By the time Blue Note began to experience a revival of interest and business, key jazz players such as Hank Mobley, Grant Green and Lee Morgan had died. Others still played: Sonny Rollins, Jimmy Smith, Lou Donaldson and Jackie McLean. Some, like pianists George Wallington and Beryl Booker as well as Jutta Hipp, were alive but had gone dormant.

•

When Tom Evered and Astrid Heppner found Hipp, she was living in a four-story walkup. The brown-brick exterior was crisscrossed by fire escapes, with air conditioning units hanging outside of windows. Apartments stood on one side of the street and a plain warehouse on the other. Inside, the building was dark. Evered and Heppner followed the hall to unit 1C and knocked on the door. Hipp answered, smiling. "I wouldn't have recognized her," Evered said. She didn't look like the smooth-skinned woman with lustrous black hair on the album covers.

The apartment was simple—just a bedroom and a sitting room—and the furniture was spare, but art decorated the walls: drawings and paintings, photos and sewing, most of which Hipp had made. "There was not a piano in the house," Evered said. It was one of the first things he noticed. He and Heppner offered to take Hipp to lunch, but she was under the weather. Instead, they sat on her sofa, and she served cake and coffee. "She was very happy that we were there," Evered said, "very personable, and she wanted to be a good hostess even though she wasn't feeling well." They talked about her royalties, talked about her paintings and drawings, talked about the cake. "She didn't have stories on the tip of her tongue about playing with various people," Evered said. "She didn't want to talk about Alfred Lion or Germany." So the conversation fluttered from one light topic to the next, and when it fizzled, Evered scrambled for things to say. "I was looking for something she might want to talk about," he said, "to make her at ease."

He'd noticed an image on her living-room wall: a framed photo of the Concorde supersonic jet. *That's strange*, he thought. The previous year, a Concorde had crashed at an airport in Paris. "Why do you have a picture of the Concorde on your wall?" he said.

"Oh," Hipp said, "I just love the looks of it. My

friends and I used to go out by JFK and sit by the Bay, and we would wait for the Concorde to take off." She had photographed it more times than she could count. She told Evered and Heppner about how much she enjoyed going to Jamaica Bay to paint watercolors and watch birds. Years later, he found out she'd sold these paintings at local street fairs. The year before his visit, some of the paintings had hung at the Langston Hughes Community Library and Cultural Center in Queens.

Evered spotted another framed item on her wall: a piece of paper on which Hipp had written important dates in her life. One of them was November 18, 1955, the day she arrived in the United States.

Even when the meeting felt labored, it never became truly awkward. "But the conversation," Tom said, "really just didn't keep going." As a jazz fan, he had a few questions he wanted to ask her, questions about who she'd played with and where she played, and if she still listened to jazz, but they were questions he didn't ask. "I didn't want to just bombard this old woman with questions," he said, "because she didn't really seem like she wanted to talk about the old days." He did ask her if she played music anymore, though, and he says he'll never forget the look on her face as she said, "Ach, no. I don't play anymore." Then she put the issue to rest in her accented English. "I wasn't very good."

"I think, sadly, that's kind of the way she judged her career," Evered said. "We, of course, disagreed, but she had made up her mind and we weren't going to argue about it." She'd just written off that part of her life. Evered found it a little disheartening. "It was sad to see somebody who turned her back on what talent she did have." Today, he looks back on the visit with regret that he didn't ask her more questions or come back and visit her again. "I kind of kick myself for not reaching out to her a little more," he said.

Evered and Heppner stayed for about an hour. "We gave her the check, and I said, 'Is there anything else I can do for you?' Because I saw how she was living—which wasn't destitute by any means, but not a lot of luxuries. She said, no, she was just happy to get this."

A week after their visit, a box of little German cookies arrived at the Blue Note office, a thank-you gift from Hipp. She and Evered spoke a few times on the phone, and she received a few more royalty checks. Two years later, she died.

She had no heirs. She wasn't in touch with her son. When she'd moved overseas, she wanted to bring her mother and brother Hajo to the United States, but that never happened, though her brother visited once a year. Hipp called him a jazz fanatic, because he spent so much of his trip sitting in her apartment, listening to jazz on local 88.3 FM. He was too sick to attend her funeral.

Hipp's apartment was cleaned, and new tenants moved in. She'd willed her body to Columbia University Medical

Center for research. In 2005, her ashes were sprinkled over one of her favorite places: Long Island Sound.

•

Four days after Hipp's death, the *New York Times* ran an obit. It provided a detailed account of her life, though it wasn't without errors. "She was living alone in Jackson Heights, Queens," the article said, getting the neighborhood wrong. Also incorrect was the line, "In 1958 she stopped playing jazz because of low self-confidence." It was more complicated than that, and anyway, she'd kept performing until 1960. But perhaps the mistakes were understandable, given how far off the cultural radar Hipp had moved. Over the years, she had declined so many interviews too. When she did finally speak about her life, it was in a 1998 interview for the now defunct *Jazz News*. It includes dates. It includes Hipp's financial reasons for retirement as well as an account of her escape from East Germany, along with other stories about her life. When the interviewer asks about moving to the United States in 1955, Hipp mentions living in Feather's house. "I had a little room," she says, "and I had to share a bathroom with a girl. The bathroom was in between us. She was from church, and she would always sing chorales. *[Laughs.]* Those were miserable times. I don't want to remember them."

She describes walking home from school one day after

Allied aircraft bombed Leipzig, how she walked for hours among burning buildings. "I didn't even know if my parents and my brother were still alive." She tells a story about the time she tried to talk to Miles Davis at a New York club, and Davis yelled, "Get the hell out of my face!" And she tells a story about riding through Brooklyn with the jazz patron "The Baroness" Pannonica de Koenigswarter, how de Koenigswarter was driving so crazily that the other passenger, singer Babs Gonzalez, said to Hipp, "Let's get out of the car," and they took the subway home.

"It's too bad that you don't play piano anymore," the interviewer says.

"No," says Hipp, "it's good that I don't because there [are] so many good piano players who are a thousand times better."

"But wouldn't you find piano playing to be relaxing?"

"Well, so is painting and listening," she says.

The interviewer then asks if she's received other requests to talk about her life and music, and all the tired issues that had shadowed her for decades rise up—issues of obscurity, of why, the same questions about the old days and what she's been doing and if she'll ever perform again. Laying it all to rest, Hipp says, "I don't really care for that. I've said everything I have to say already."

When It Was New:
Miles Davis' 'So What'

Four weeks after first recording "So What" on March 2nd, 1959, Miles Davis' band recorded the song again in a Manhattan TV studio. Shot for a thirty-minute episode of CBS's short-lived *Roy Herridge Theater* series, the footage aired as *The Sounds of Miles Davis*, an episode dedicated to the trumpeter's music and broadcast during the era of his skyrocketing fame. What makes this televised version significant isn't simply the way it captures the first recorded public performance of one of jazz's most beloved compositions. Nor is it that the band plays the song without alto saxophonist Cannonball Adderley (he was sick with a migraine), or that pianist Wynton Kelly takes the place of pianist Bill Evans, although those elements do contribute. What's significant is its feel.

To my ears, the emotional power and melodicism of Davis and Coltrane's solos match those of the originals on *Kind of Blue*, which isn't something I can say about most of the live recordings Davis' bands made of "So What" in the decade that followed. The fact that we have two equally inspired versions of this canonical song, from the month of its birth, confirms and complicates what seems the simple idea behind Davis' approach to the album: that first takes are best takes. It also shows how right Davis was about the connection between improvisation and newness. He knew that a certain lack of familiarity with the material could improve a soloist's ingenuity, and that band leaders were wise to create conditions which fostered this relationship.

Like his mentor and old band mate Charlie Parker, Miles believed, as biographer Ian Carr put it, that "the most creative and dynamic solos occurred on the first takes". "I've recorded with Miles," said trombonist J. J. Johnson, "and I know how he operates. Most of the time he goes into the studio and one take is it! Goofs or not, there's no second or third take." When Davis took his sextet in to record *Kind of Blue*, he pushed the first take philosophy even further.

The legend has Davis arriving at the studio with a few rough song sketches jotted down. The engineer rolls tape, and each musician nails their moving, inventive solos on the first try, while essentially learning each tune. In the album's original liner notes, Bill Evans encourages this perception when he says, "Miles conceived these settings only hours before the recording dates." The truth is more complex.

The album is composed not of first tries, but of, with one exception, first full takes. Davis arrived at the studio with certain songs loosely charted. Some, like "Freddie Freeloader" and "So What," weren't written down at all. He gave his musicians scant directions, sometimes about where to solo, sometimes about the type of drum beat to play. Unlike most sessions, the band never formally rehearsed the material; yet the material wasn't entirely new to them either.

The song "All Blues" developed during a few months of live performance. Bill Evans composed part of "Blue in Green" and "Flamenco Sketches," though the amount is debated. And according to drummer Jimmy Cobb, before the recording session, the band "had played ['So What'] once or twice on gigs." Despite this rough preparation and vague familiarity with certain tunes, spontaneity still defines the album. What you hear on record are performances electrified by the anxiety and excitement of discovery, of musicians fumbling and fretting and figuring out each song's melodic potential and essential character as they went. This is what Davis wanted: songs composed of improvised passages, where off-the-cuff solos, as much as ensembles or prepared themes, defined the composition.

As Cannonball Adderely explained it, Miles was "tired of *tunes*." In Be Bop and into its successor Hard bop, the standard jazz song had musicians playing the song's theme. Each musician then took a turn to solo, moving through a limited number of chord changes, before returning to the theme to wrap it up. Miles wanted more. "A solo is the way he thinks about the composition, and the solo became *the* thing," said Adderley. "He thinks a solo can be a composition if it's expressed the right way." Davis' first take philosophy helped make that happen on *Kind of Blue*. It wasn't the first time.

In order to satisfy contractual obligations in 1956, Davis famously took his quintet into the studio on two separate days and recorded enough material for four albums: *Workin'*, *Steamin'*, *Cookin'* and *Relaxin'*. The material is timeless. Many fans consider it some of jazz's best. In addition to the personnel and set lists, what animates these sessions is the approach: they're live albums, recorded without overdubs or second takes. The band had played these tunes numerous times—it was essentially their working repertoire—so the material wasn't unfamiliar in the way that the *Kind of Blue* material was when they recorded it. But by trusting his musicians' instincts, Davis' first take, best take philosophy captured his band as they sounded in clubs, and he provided undeniable examples of the way the pressure and freedom of live performance can yield exalted, imaginative solos.

If *Kind of Blue* displays the strengths of the first take philosophy, then the life history of "So What" provides a window into the flipside of improvisation: the way continued live performance can inhibit innovation and yield less imaginative, or at least less appealing, solos.

The CBS TV footage marked the beginning of the song's inclusion in Davis' live set list. From 1959 to 1969, Davis' bands regularly performed the song in concert. It was popular. In the spring of 1960, Davis played it night after night in Europe with Coltrane, Jimmy Cobb, Paul Chambers and Wynton Kelly. After Coltrane left, saxophonist Hank Mobley filled the tenor slot and played "So What" with Davis. And when Miles replaced his old band with a new one containing Herbie Hancock and Ron Carter in 1963, they played "So What" all over the world. In the case of this song, Davis gave audiences what they wanted, though not in the form they might have craved.

Each new musician altered the band dynamic, as did Davis' own ever-changing interests. These factors combine to make the live versions of "So What" a map of the trumpeter's continuing evolution: from modal jazz and Hard bop, to a more free form experimentation that led him to fusion. In the process of evolving, Davis so thoroughly transforms the song that the mid-60s versions almost demand a different title than the 1959 and 1960 ones.

Listen to 1961 "So What" recorded with Mobley at Carnegie Hall. Listen to the take with Hancock and Carter from *Live at the 1963 Monterey Jazz Festival*, and the 1964 takes from Lincoln Center on *Four & More*, 1964 Tokyo and Berlin, and the Plugged Nickel in 1965. The post-Coltrane versions are faster. The percussion becomes more forceful, polyrhythmic and free-ranging, often raucous and messy. Davis and the tenors after Mobley aren't playing in the Hard bop idiom so much as playing a decorously avant-garde, sometimes aggressive style in a post-Ornette

Coleman world. There's a loosening of conventions in these later versions, less interest in melody, standard rhythms and traditional harmonic progression. Although it's not truly free jazz, the music often sounds a lot like it.

Now listen to the versions from CBS television and *Kind of Blue*. The tempos are slower, the drumming simpler, more ventilated. Both takes are poignant and moody, and they contain the strengths of many of Davis' best mid-century solos and ballads: lyricism, grace, melody laced with darkness and sensitivity, composed as much by the notes he plays as by the spaces he leaves between them. This is why they resonate with me.

The longer Davis performed "So What," the less emotionally engaging it became. Although the basic song structure seemed to remain interesting to the musicians as a forum for experimentation and point of departure, repeat live performance was also a form of emotional dilution— if not the opposite of the improvisational freshness that Miles sought in studio, then at least a process that inhibited the profound, expressive moods of the originals. In other words, the first takes were the best takes. The later soloists are still improvising, just in a different way than when the song was in its infancy. They're not exploring a new composition to see where they can take it melodically so much as testing the nature and meaning of jazz itself. As a listener, I find that less appealing.

Reviewing Davis' 1965 album *E.S.P.* for *Down Beat*

magazine, trumpeter Kenny Dorham inadvertently articulated the problem: "I like to rate albums in the way that they move me emotionally as well as otherwise. Emotionally, as a whole, this one is lacking. It's mostly brain music. ...*E.S.P.* music in general is monotonous—one long drone. It's not for me." What Miles said in the *Sketches of Spain* liner notes applies as much to his approach to that album as it does to the inadequacies Dorham references. "It was hard to get the musicians to realize that they didn't have to play perfect," Davis wrote. "It was the feeling that counted." Even though feeling clearly mattered to Davis, later versions of "So What" contain so little of it. They're mostly brain music.

How you react to Dorham's and my assessments reveals less about the quality of the songs as it does about you as a listener. Tell me which versions of "So What" you like, and I'll tell you what kind of jazz fan you are. Do you prefer the avant-garde or the swinging stuff? The bluesy, gospel-infused back beat of Hard bop, or cleaner, brassier, funkier ensembles? Ornette Coleman or Coleman Hawkins? Oscar Peterson or Thelonious Monk? Of course, you can like them all. More often than not, Ornette fans find Hawkins ordinary or outdated, and Monk fans find Peterson lacking a certain fire and angularity. (In the world of distilled spirits, people often say that you either like Scotch or bourbon, but not both. I like both, just specific kinds.) The issue of "So What" is a matter of taste not quality, because it isn't the same song across the years. It's played not only by different musicians, but different Miles Davises.

Some fans and critics like to say that Davis played "So What" so fast in the '60s because he'd grown bored with it; he performed it out of obligation to concert goers, but sped the tempo to get it over with. Whether or not that's true, by the time he hired Hancock and Carter, he'd lost interest in many of the ideas that went into the recording of *Kind of Blue*. He wasn't modal Miles anymore. He was interested in what he and Hancock called "controlled freedom"—not quite free jazz, but equally exploratory in its defiance of tradition. Davis was always changing. "I have to change," he once said. "It's like a curse." The live versions of "So What" chart specifically *how* he changed.

As Hancock described the band, "[W]hen people were hearing us, they were hearing the avant-garde on the one hand, and they were hearing the history of jazz that led up [to] it on the other hand—because Miles was that history. He was that link." So too with "So What." The song bridged the post-Bop and free jazz eras, combining the mix of tradition and reinvention that defined those revolutionary times in jazz and American society. "So What" was effectively an artifact from Davis' previous identity. He no longer played it how the band first composed it, because he was no longer the same person. As a listener, I'm still not into it.

To me, the later versions don't completely lack feeling

so much as lack the feelings that I gravitate to in jazz. I like early and middle Freddie Hubbard and Jackie McLean, not later. I like blues and gospel, prefer Art Blakey and Horace Silver to Sam Rivers or Andrew Hill. And my Miles is *Workin'* and *Milestones* Miles, not *Nefertiti* or *Bitches Brew*. Although the 1961 version of "So What" recorded at the Blackhawk Supper Club in San Francisco is often hailed as a classic, I find it more chaotic than emotive. The strongest feeling it induces is frazzled nerves. Same with the Lincoln Center and Plugged Nickel performances. To me, they're too fast, too frantic, the solos too showy. Flash and verbosity take the place of melody and emotion. Where *Kind of Blue* and Davis' mid-50s style scaled back the clutter and speed of Be Bop and highlighted his lyricism, the mid-60s saw speed and clutter return to his performances, a concern with pyrotechnics rather than the lyricism of economy. I'm with Dorham: "It's not for me."

At a March, 1969 concert at Duffy's Backstage in Rochester, New York, Davis performed "So What" for the last time. It seems safe to assume he'd tired of it, since whenever he changed, he rarely looked back at his previous work, and he'd changed a lot by then. As he told *The Jazz Times* in 1986: "'So What' or Kind of Blue, they were done in that era, the right hour, the right day, and it happened. It's over [...]. What I used to play with Bill Evans, all those different modes, and substitute chords, we had the energy then and we liked it. But I have no feel for it anymore—

it's more like warmed-over turkey." If he had "no feel for" the song anymore, we might take that to mean he no longer found it stimulating to experiment with, or that he no longer even found it bearable to perform by rote. A mapped frontier offers few opportunities for exploration, and pioneers like Davis are only interested in exploration. According to one exhaustive Miles Davis fan site, he'd performed "Bye Bye Blackbird" live for seven years before retiring it, "Now's the Time" for ten. As he said, *Kind of Blue* was done at "the right hour, the right day", which is the essence of a first take: a single, ephemeral convergence of factors, whose energy and dynamics you cannot recreate and have to let go of once they dissipate.

Like most of his songs, "So What" held the most interest for him during the beginning of his relationship with it, and I, as a listener, can hear his interest peak and wane. Maybe I'm reading into it. Maybe I'm hearing boredom where there are only stylistic shifts. I don't think so. Whatever his reasons, Davis struck the song from his set list, exactly ten years after he first recorded it, and moved onto the next thing, just as he should.

What Is and What Could Be: Hank Mobley

When my coworker Robert heard that I was getting into jazz, he brought a CD into work for me. "You need this," he said smiling. He slid the jewel case across the dusty top of my computer terminal. It was Hank Mobley's *Soul Station*.

Set against a black background, beneath three rows of simple text, Mobley's face and shoulders hovered in the center of the album cover, a statuary bust awash in aquamarine. "He looks like he's high out of his mind," Robert said. It was true. Head back, eyes hidden beneath heavy lids, the young tenor wore a euphoric smirk whose mix of bliss and self-assurance seemed to dare you to ask what he was so ecstatic about. But what if he wasn't high, just ecstatic? Couldn't this be a smile of satisfaction and excitement, the pure childlike reverie musicians feel when playing stirring music in a well-equipped studio? Although I didn't know it then, Mobley had had drug problems off and on—many jazz players had—but at the time of this recording, he was as clear as his polished horn. You can hear it in the music. This album is his masterpiece. That's why it's fitting that he holds up his saxophone in triumph on the cover.

•

In 1979, at age forty-nine, Mobley told journalist John Litweiler, "It's hard for me to think of what could be and what should have been. I lived with Charlie Parker, Bud Powell, Thelonious Monk; I walked with them up and down the street. I did not know what it meant when I listened to them cry—until it happened to me."

The first time I read these sentences, they filled me with gloom. The thought of one of my favorite tenors suffering enough to cry left me grieving into the night. It also raised the question: What happened to Mobley?

What "should have been"—*should have*. Should. 'Should' is the language of outcomes. The word suggests a blueprint of the mechanics behind fate, about our conceptions of fairness, providence and stakes, as well as a person's expectations, not just what we're entitled to, but about how much we believe in the American value of "hard work + time = rewards & improvement." In its grandest application, 'should' can suggest the inner workings of cosmic justice, what the universe owes you—reward for effort, reward for morality, Karmic recompense. Here, the word delivers news of destiny undelivered. What Mobley thought should have happened did not. Instead, he got something else, something that seems to have challenged his worldview and suffused it with some amount of regret.

Mobley's words remind me of the song, "It Could Happen to You." Like many Be Bop and Hard bop standards, this one debuted as a vocal number in a film, the 1944 musical *And the Angels Sing*, but numerous musicians in Mobley's day played instrumental versions of it.

"Hide your heart from sight, lock your dreams at night," go the lyrics. "It could happen to you. Don't count stars or you might stumble. Someone drops a sigh and down you tumble."

Thanks to biographies and Hollywood archetypes, we know the typical tragedies of the working musician: creative freedom without financial stability; cult status without widespread recognition; health problems but no health insurance. Thanks to jazz lore, we know the others' particular tragedies: Charlie Parker's self-destructive genius; Bud Powell's groundbreaking vision interrupted by mental illness; Monk's imagination and compositions, beloved by insiders but unable to generate the money or fame deserving of his brilliance. Mobley never enjoyed their distinction or profile, yet what happened to him was the same as the others: Bad luck and trouble, the currency of the Blues, and like Charlie Parker taught him, "Baby, you'd better learn those blues; can't play enough of the blues."

•

The song "Remember" on *Soul Station* starts with some of the most joyous jazz on record, forty-five seconds of pure, swinging elation.

Out front, Mobley's sax plays the theme: very spare, very simple. Pianist Wynton Kelly laces the theme with bright, jubilant chords tapped with the weight of angel food cake. Behind them, drummer Art Blakey's swift beat moves the intro along until he marks the end with one of his thunderous press rolls, and kicks off Mobley's two-minute solo with a brassy cymbal crash.

"Remember" is a cover of an Irving Berlin song, one that appeared in 1925 with melancholy lyrics.

Remember we found a lonely spot,
And after I learned to care a lot,
You promised that you'd forget me not,
But you forgot
To remember.

Yet on *Soul Station* stripped of lyrics, the song loses its mournful theme and becomes something so joyful, it sounds the way falling in love feels. The band transforms a eulogy to lost love into an anthem of elation, infusing it with a sense of optimism and excitement which, in the soundtrack to an unwritten film in my mind, seems to signal the arrival of new beginnings, a farewell to hardship and hello to something epic. The hippity-hop of Kelly's piano,

Mobley's round, lush tone and Blakey's buoyant shuffle—
if you want a glimpse into a happy soul, into how I feel on
my best days, those forty-five seconds of music are it.

I've listened to "Remember" so many times that when
I sing along with Mobley's solo, I know nearly every note
he plays. I know when Blakey intensifies the beat, when
he changes the rhythm, and I know all his fills. I can sing
Kelly's ebullient solo, and I know the spots where you can
hear Kelly humming to himself—something he often did—
as well as the spots where he heightens the mood by hitting
the keys harder. This isn't a boast about my sophisticated
ear. It's a tribute to how melodic and infectious the music
is. So melodic, so cleanly articulated and composed, that
even a guy like me who plays one instrument poorly can
remember it.

> Remember the night
> The night you said, "I love you."
> Remember?
> Remember you vowed
> By all the stars above you.
> Remember?

I remember walking up Manhattan's Park Avenue in the
winter of 2007, listening to this song. The sun had nearly
set. A steely blue encased the street, the towering buildings
and expansive pavement all bearing the same cool color as

the inside of your eyelids at dawn. Mobley's "Remember" played in my earphones, and it washed me with a feeling of confidence and calm. I shuffled through the frigid air and stopped at the curb on 39th. Cars raced past. I waited for a gap. When I looked down at my cheap cotton shoes, the toes were wet and perched on the worn cement edge, and instead of bemoaning how cold and tired and wet I felt, I thought, "I feel good." I was aware of it at that moment, and I knew that the song was the reason.

I only lived in New York for one year, but "Remember," like all of *Soul Station*, was one of the only energizing forces during that period of fatigue. More than all the coffee and tea I drank to combat sleep-deprivation, more than the endless amounts of nicotine I consumed to feel better about stress and lack of money, cold weather, exhaustion and wet shoes, that album powered me through. It so effectively cushioned the blows my life dealt that, when I think about that year now, I hear this song and mostly remember the good things that happened, the overall tone of it, which is the tone this song set.

Part of the charm of "Remember" is its pace. The beat is perfectly spaced so that when your legs move in sync with it, it sets you sashaying up the street. When Blakey struts, you strut. When Kelly swings, you swing. It's the ideal song for walking, because the song's confidence and swagger infuses the listener, and as you move to keep pace, you temporarily inhabit its joyous disposition.

As writer Bob Blumenthal says in the remastered *Soul Station* liner notes, "All six [songs] are delivered with a natural ease that may create a misleading impression of easy music—what could sound easier, for instance, than the opening choruses of 'Remember?'—yet that is part of the brilliance behind the album. If everybody could toss off music this satisfying, then *Soul Station* would have far more company at the pinnacle of recorded jazz."

> Into my dreams you wandered it seems, and then
> there came a day
> You loved me too, my dreams had come true, and all
> the world was May
> But soon the May-time turned to December
> You had forgotten, do you remember?

It takes talents like Kelly, Blakey and Mobley to perform music this satisfying, but how did they make such a sad song so uplifting?

•

"Where do you think everybody got the blues from?" Mobley told *Down Beat* magazine in 1973. "Did you ever hear *Just Friends* and tap your foot to it? *Soul Station* is the same thing, just like walking down the highway, it sounds like somebody's saying, 'Oh, man, I'm tired of this town, got to get away from this."

Born in Georgia in 1930, Mobley started playing sax at age sixteen after his family moved to New Jersey. A few relatives played instruments. He learned piano as a kid, but alto captured his attention. When he spotted one at a local store, he saved up money by working at a bowling alley. "When I finally got up enough money for my horn, the dealer went on a month's vacation," Mobley said. "In the meantime, I got a music book, and when he got back, I knew the whole instrument; all I had to do was put it in my mouth and play. I'll tell you, when I was about 8 they wanted me to play the piano, but I wanted to play cops and robbers. But when I got serious the music started coming easy."

"I was in woodshop, carpentry, auto mechanics; then I took machine shop for a year. I was a nervous wreck studying to be a machinist. We had a little music thing in school, and I played this Lester Young solo, *One O'Clock Jump*, note for note. The shop teacher used to play trumpet, and he said, 'There's no room out there for a black machinist. The way you play saxophone, why don't you study that?' That's the way I did. I quit shop that same year, I just put on my hip clothes and went chasing women and going to rock and roll things…"

His uncle played seven instruments, including trumpet, and even briefly led his own band. "My uncle told me a lot of things," Mobley said, "and he always used to say,

'Listen to Lester Young.' When I was about 18 he told me: 'If you're playing with somebody who plays loud, you play soft. If somebody plays fast, you play slow. If you try to play the same thing they're playing you're in trouble.' Contrast. If you play next to Johnny Griffin or Coltrane, that's hard work. You have to out-psych them. They'd say, 'Let's play *Cherokee*,' I'd go, 'naw, naw—ah, how about a little *Bye Bye Blackbird?*' I put my heavy form on them, then I can double up and do everything I want to do."

This contrast served him well. In an era of speeding solos, he became a master of mid-tempo, but only after years of playing professionally. First, he switched instruments. "To the best of my knowledge," he said, "Sonny Rollins, Sonny Stitt, myself, Jimmy Heath, John Coltrane—we called ourselves the 'Five Brothers', you know, the five *black* brothers—we all started playing alto, but Charlie Parker was such a monster that we all gave up and switched to tenor. I wasn't creating anything new, I was just part of a clique. When we all listened to Fats Navarro and Bud Powell, when we were 20, 21, all of us were learning together. We weren't trying to surpass Parker or the heavyweights. But as you get older you start finding different directions. At the time it was like going to college. It was just doing our thing, playing different changes, experimenting . . ."

Based solely on Mobley's reputation, trumpeter Clifford Brown recommended him for a job with Newark-based

R&B pianist Paul Gayten, in 1949. Brown had never even heard Mobley play. After two years with Gayten, Mobley left to join the house band at a Newark club, alongside pianist Walter Davis Jr. Every week, some of jazz's biggest names came from New York to perform, and Mobley backed them: Miles Davis, Billie Holiday, Bud Powell. After one weekend show at the club in 1951, drummer Max Roach hired him and Walter Davis. "I was just 21," said Mobley. "We opened in a place on 125th Street in Harlem; Charlie Parker had just been there before me, and here I come. I'm scared to death—here's Sonny Rollins, Jackie McLean, Kenny Dorham, Gerry Mulligan, just about all the young musicians came by there." That gig launched his career.

Mobley and Davis recorded with Roach in early 1953 on one of the drummer's first dates as a leader. He recorded on other Roach albums and played with others whose names are now legendary: Tadd Dameron, Milt Jackson, J.J. Johnson. He did two weeks with Duke Ellington's orchestra in 1953 when their clarinetist and tenor Jimmy Hamilton stepped out to get some dental work. He spent the next year playing and recording with Dizzy Gillespie and then joined drummer Art Blakey and pianist Horace Silver in a band that became one of jazz's most influential, some of the architects of Hard bop, The Jazz Messengers. Considered a classic, their debut album, *Horace Silver and the Jazz Messengers*, was one of the earliest Hard bop sessions, and it announced the tone for the post-Bop era, as well as

Art Blakey's career, since he carried the Jazz Messengers name for the next thirty-five years of his life.

The Messengers started out as a collective of friends pooling their resources and playing what they liked. "Horace had the quartet at Minton's," Mobley said, "then on weekends Art Blakey and Kenny Dorham would come in to jam, 'cause they were right around the corner. Out of that we started feeling something, and we said, 'Let's do our thing; we all got something going name-wise; if anyone gets a job let's use all of us.' I think [drummer] Arthur Edgehill was working with somebody else, too, but Blakey was right there. Horace'd get a job, or Art, or Kenny, or I'd get a job; we'd split the money equally."

Charlie Parker didn't give formal lessons to young players or mentor them; he threw them bits of advice, and he advised the young Mobley to learn the blues. Besides being a genre of music and specific chord progressions, 'the blues' is also code for trouble, for suffering, sadness and misfortune. "Parker played the *modern* blues," Mobley said, "what he's saying is that so much of modern jazz, structures, harmonic progressions, they're all based on the blues." He also embodied it. Brilliant, charming, inventive, self-destructive, in Bop, Parker helped create a new type of music, and before he died at age thirty-four from drug and alcohol abuse, his music and lifestyle led countless players to the horn and the needle.

Between the year of Parker's death and 1958, Mobley

recorded nine albums as a leader for Blue Note Records, four for other labels, and he played as a sideman on numerous others. Those Blue Note sessions at Rudy Van Gelder's studio were salad days. "They'd buy the whiskey and brandy Saturday night and the food on Sunday—they'd set out salami, liverwurst, bologna, rye bread, the whole bit," said Mobley, "Only Blue Note did it; the others [Prestige and Savoy] were a little stiff." Blue Note was equally generous with rehearsals. Because they wanted solid albums, they paid for musicians' practice. "If we had a date Saturday, I'd rehearse the band Tuesday and Thursday in a New York studio…"

During his career, Mobley recorded as a leader almost exclusively for Blue Note, a label run by Alfred Lion and Francis Wolff, two German immigrants whose jazz fanaticism and impeccable taste speak to their players' abilities. Lion and Wolff were meticulous. They had strong opinions about what did and didn't sound good, and they mostly recorded what they liked rather that what they thought would sell. "We'd be making a tape, and sometimes my horn might squeak, and Frank Wolff would say, 'Hank Mobley! You squeaked! You squeaked!'—and the whole band would crack up, we couldn't get back to play the tune. And old Alfred Lion would be walking around, (*snap*) 'Mmm!' (*snap*) 'Ooh!' (*snap*)—'Now vait a minute, it don't sving, it don't sving!' So we'd stop and laugh, then come back and slow it down just a bit. Then he'd say, (snap)

(snap), 'Fine, fine, dot really svings, ja!'"

By the mid-50s, Mobley had grown as a composer since his Newark days, with some of his strongest early material appearing on *Hank Mobley Quartet*, *Hank Mobley Quintet* and *Hank Mobley and His All-Stars*. By the time he released *Peckin' Time* in 1958, a deepening heroin dependence led to his arrest, though, and the prison sentence kept him out of music for most of the year. When he returned in 1959, he briefly rejoined Art Blakey and the Jazz Messengers to reestablish his bearings, and he got right back to recording. *Soul Station* was his comeback. As Bob Blumenthal says in the remastered liner notes, drug problems "interrupted his performing career, yet, as the recorded evidence proves, they had not impeded his progress." He followed the album with a string of powerful records the following year, *Roll Call*, *Workout* and *Another Workout*, creating a sequence that inarguably compose the best of his oeuvre.

In 1961, Miles Davis punctuated Mobley's winning streak with what seemed the opportunity of a lifetime: to play in his quintet. Davis led one of jazz's most popular outfits. He paid his musicians well. They had frequent bookings and lots of press. For a brief time, Davis even paid a retainer to make sure his musicians were available when he needed them. "That was the best job you could have," said Davis' drummer Jimmy Cobb, "about as high as you could get playing jazz music, so I was feeling pretty good about it." Davis' visibility also launched John

Coltrane's, Red Garland's and Cannonball Adderley's solo careers. When Coltrane left to focus on his own songwriting and recording, the trumpeter went searching for the right replacement. He wanted Sonny Rollins, but Rollins had taken a sabbatical. He wanted Jimmy Heath, but parole limited the distance Heath could travel to perform. He hired Mobley. After less than a year together, the association dissolved.

"[P]laying with Hank just wasn't fun for me," Davis said in his autobiography, "he didn't stimulate my imagination". The problem was stylistic. Mobley's style was too laid back, too legato and behind the beat. Davis could also be cruel. He often hassled his new musicians by comparing them with the musicians whose slots they'd filled. He did this to Cobb, did it to Red Garland, and he did it to Mobley. During one concert, while Mobley soloed, Miles stood within earshot and said, "Any time Sonny Rollins shows up with his horn, he's got the job." The tenor eventually quit. "But when I left Miles [in 1961]," he said, "I was so tired of music, the whole world, man, I just went back to drugs."

He played a few sessions, some his own like the darkly melodic *No Room for Squares*, some for others like organist Freddie Roach. In 1964, he got arrested for narcotics again and imprisoned. He wrote the songs for the octet that became *Slice of the Top* and had to give pianist Duke Pearson the sheet music to arrange while he served prison time. Like before, Mobley didn't let his problems slow him down. During the second half of the 1960s, he managed to record an album or more for Blue Note every year: *Far Away Lands*, *High Voltage*, *Third Season*, *The Flip*. These albums are dense and listenable, featuring some catchy, complex, standout tunes, but they aren't as potent as *Soul Station* or *Workout*. He lived in Chicago for a while and led a band with pianist Muhal Richard Abrams and drummer Wilbur Campbell. He married Arlene Lisser, an assistant professor of psychiatry at University of Illinois, and a fan. Once he and Lisser split, he left Chicago. Rather than enter an Alcohol Treatment Unit, he moved, living briefly in East Orange, New Jersey, then in Philadelphia, where his health deteriorated.

When *Slice of the Top* finally came out in 1979, thirteen years after it was recorded, Mobley was forty-nine and in bad shape. As the text on the record sleeve says, he had two lung operations in the early-70s, which kept him from performing or recording. A problem with a birth certificate kept him from participating in a European festival. And he had two of his saxophones stolen. The one sax he had leaked, so the sound was off, and he didn't have the money to buy a replacement. Not that it mattered. "The doctor told me not to play it, or I might blow one of my lungs out," he said. By 1975, he was effectively retired, a fate undeserved for a musician of his achievement and ability.

As he said on the record sleeve, "It's hard for me to think of what could be and what should have been. I lived with Charlie Parker, Bud Powell, Thelonious Monk; I walked with them up and down the street. I did not know what it meant when I listened to them cry—until it happened to me." Maybe I'm misreading it or taking it out of context, but when I read those words, I hear a person looking back not just on their career, but on their life. *Did I waste it? Where did it get me?* After so many fruitful decades, here he was on life's leeward slope, taking stock of his vanished youth.

You can feel the reflection and fear in his voice, the question of meaning. *Look at all the things I did*, he seems to be saying, *all the places I went and people I knew.* All the practice. All the time spent composing, playing gigs, losing sleep to write and rehearse and record twenty-five albums for Blue Note, all the hustling. Playing alongside Parker and Monk, helping start The Jazz Messengers, playing with Max Roach before he formed his famous band, filling in for Coltrane in Miles' quintet—he'd been in nearly all the right places at the right time, everywhere any tenor would want to be. *Shouldn't it have amounted to more?* But Mobley's pianist on *Soul Station*, Wynton Kelly, died of a seizure in Canada at age thirty-nine, broke. Mobley's old Jazz Messengers bassist Doug Watkins died at age twenty-eight in a car accident, the same tragic end that the clean-living, twenty-five year old trumpeter Clifford Brown met, the person who got Mobley his first job. And his trumpeter friend and collaborator Lee Morgan? A jealous lover shot him on stage at a show when he was thirty-three. In music and life, there is no justice. Mobley's final album offers evidence of this.

Blue Note's cofounder Francis Wolff died in 1971, and the company, like jazz, changed. The following year, Mobley teamed up with pianist Cedar Walton and recorded *Breakthrough!* for a small label named Muse. It was the first album he'd done as a leader for another company since 1955, and it looks the part. An oversized image of a cinder block floats on the cover, a grainy grey CGI set against the sort of blown-out, artificially blue sky that you find in allergy medicine commercials. There's no expressive profile of the artist. No careful font or lush coloration. Everything about the cover suggests an afterthought, as if the label saw Mobley as some hobbyist from the burbs who'd just learned the horn, and treated this not as another in a sequence of solid sessions, but as a throwaway. In hindsight, this album stands as a capstone to one of jazz's great careers. Based on the cover, it resembles a vanity project.

Why the title "Breakthrough"? Break through to what, death? The other side? Judging from the album's low production values, the title could not have been suggesting that Mobley was finally going to break through the barrier of popular appreciation and earn him the recognition he deserved. Although Mobley hadn't "broken through" to fame, he had already made his name and left his mark, had broken and rebroken if measured by his triumphs over adversity. Instead of encouraging, the title reads like an ignorant assessment of his career, patronizing even, in the same way that his last Blue Note album, *Thinking of Home*, inadvertently reads like cruel commentary on his physical frailty, a way to point out the low sad station of his soul in old age, a curtain call—which is another one of his album titles—as if God Himself were calling him home. Fortunately, the music on *Breakthrough!* isn't as awful as the presentation. As Scott Yanow at Allmusic says, "Hank...is in brilliant form, showing how much he had grown since his earlier days." His solo on "Summertime" is particularly emotive. After it, he recorded nothing more.

After somehow managing to work briefly with pianist Duke Jordan in Philadelphia in 1986, Mobley died of pneumonia in May of that year. He spent the last years of his life so far off the radar that even the attentive *New York Times* failed to notice his passing and issue an obituary.

In his heyday, musicians and listeners appreciated Mobley for his songwriting and melodic playing, yet he was still overshadowed by more assertive or inventive players. Noted critic Leonard Feather inadvertently gave Mobley a demeaning tag that stayed with him his whole life, when he called him "middleweight champion of the tenor saxophone." Feather meant to describe Mobley's tone as laying somewhere between cool jazz tenors like Stan Getz and more bold players such as John Coltrane and Ornette Coleman. Instead, the metaphor implied a middling quality, a style unexceptional and middle of the road, which seems to have cast Mobley into his lifelong station as "an underrated" tenor. Even as an underdog, he earned a cult following.

In *Blue Note Records: The Biography*, author Richard Cook says, "Mobley has always been a favourite among Blue Note collectors—perhaps *the* musicians in such circles. Though a journeyman rather than any kind of ground-breaking voice, he was more influential than jazz historians have often allowed. Many British musicians of the fifties and sixties would seek out his elusive records. If a figure such as Sonny Rollins was too overpowering a voice to be useful as an influence, the more diplomatic Mobley could offer more practical material to work with."

It's tempting to say he "should have been" more famous, but to use the phrase is to face the fact that the last years of Mobley's life conflict with the jubilance and celebratory swagger of *Soul Station*. As a fan who listens to his music almost weekly, his words continue to haunt me, though not in the way they did initially.

He says he found it just as hard to think of "what should have been" as "what could be." *Could be*—that's not the language of loss. It's the language of hope. A person gazing into the future and imagining its potential is someone who thinks they'll be around in the future, someone with at least some momentary optimism. By the end of his career, he'd penned over eighty songs. Maybe at age forty-nine, he was still imagining what new songs he could write, where his music could take him, what sort of tenor he still could be. Granted, when he said "what could be" was "hard to think about," he might have meant that pessimistically: that when he thought about the future, he thought about limitations, not about what he could do so much as what he could no longer do, what could *not* be. Then again, when he said 'hard,' he might have meant 'challenging' rather than 'painful,' implying that it stretched his imagination to think about, rather than pained him. When he looked into his future, what did he see? We'll never know. His words will always carry a dual meaning, just as his posture does on *Soul Station*.

Looking at the album cover now, the way he raises his sax still seems triumphant. The truth is, it's impossible to tell. Was he raising it when Francis Wolff snapped the photo, or was he lowering it? The horn rests on the back of Mobley's shoulder, frozen between ascent and descent, action and rest, ambition and accomplishment. Behind that euphoric smirk, he could be thinking, *Man, this session is poppin'! Let's keep it going,* or he could be thinking, *Alright guys, let's call it a day and head home.* The direction of movement will forever be unclear, though it's tempting to assign meaning when you consider the direction his life took after the session. Then again, maybe he wasn't raising or lowering his saxophone at all. Maybe it's just relaxing on

his shoulder, going neither up nor down, forever brassy
and clear, and forever at rest.

Eulogy for Lee

In 1965, celebrated jazz trumpeter Lee Morgan released the song "Speedball" on his album *The Gigolo*. A year earlier, the title track from his album *The Sidewinder* had become the biggest hit in Blue Note Records' history, reaching number 25 on the *Billboard* LP charts, even appearing on a Chrysler TV commercial during the World Series. Although "Speedball" never attained the commercial success of "The Sidewinder," it endures as one of Morgan's best-known originals, and, with the possible exception of Art Pepper's album *Smack Up*, its title serves as the most barefaced allusion to the monkey on mid-century jazz's back.

Drugs, risk, rebellion—this unholy trinity seems more evocative of rock and roll longhairs than clean cut men in suits, yet these dark elements remain central to the jazzman archetype established by Charlie Parker. Between the mid-40s and early-60s, tons of talented players were strung out: Art Blakey, Hank Mobley, Sonny Rollins, Miles Davis, Grant Green, Dexter Gordon, Jackie McLean, John Coltrane. If Coltrane later provided a countervailing archetype—the sober, spiritually aware, gentle genius— then Parker embodied creativity's menacing, consumptive side. Morgan got lost between these poles. A promising, prodigy it-kid, he received his first trumpet at age thirteen. Five years later, he joined the Dizzy Gillespie Big Band. That same year, in 1956, he recorded his first Blue Note album as a leader, and soon after played on now legendary recordings such as Coltrane's *Blue Train*, at age nineteen, and Art Blakey's *Moanin'*, at twenty. His own early output ranks as nothing short of astonishing—eleven albums as a leader by age twenty-two—which is why his 1961 departure from Blakey's Jazz Messengers takes on the sinister weight of an omen.

Morgan returned to his hometown of Philadelphia to kick heroin. When he returned to New York in 1963, he recorded his comeback album, *The Sidewinder* and, clean and sober, entered his most productive period, recording seventeen Blue Note albums over the next eight years, albums that featured the songs with which he will forever be connected, including "Ceora" and "Speedball." But the trouble implied in that title never left him.

On February 19, 1972, Morgan was performing at an East Village jazz club called Slug's. He and his longtime girlfriend, Helen More, had an argument between sets, possibly about Morgan's infidelity, possibly about him trying to break up with her. Accounts vary. One has Morgan wrapping up a conversation with some people while his band waited for him on stage. Another account, from one of Morgan's close friends, and quoted in David

Rosenthal's book *Hard Bop*, has the trumpeter sitting at the bar between sets, having a drink with his new, young, attractive girlfriend. When More came up to speak to him, he led her over to a table and told her to stay there, then he headed back to the bar. More tried to talk to him again. "This time," says his friend, "Lee took her by the shoulders and, without her overcoat or anything, marched her over to the door and put her out in the cold." The temperature was five below zero. She had Lee's pistol in her pocketbook.

In the first account, Morgan climbs onto the bandstand to perform, and More calls his name from the front of the club. Lee turns to face her, and she shoots him in the chest in front of everybody. When she aims the pistol at the doorman, he grabs her wrist and snatches the gun, then she starts to scream, "Baby, what have I done?" and runs toward Morgan. In *Hard Bop*, Morgan's friend says that when More came back inside the club, she aimed the gun and shot Lee straight through the heart. "A little red stain came up on his shirt," his friend says. "Then she realized what had happened and she was crying and hanging over him and screaming 'Mogie'—that was what she called him—'what have I done?'" Whatever went down, one thing is clear: she shot him, and he died within minutes. He was thirty-three.

This Is

On February 19, 2007, jazz pianist Freddie Redd performed *The Connection* soundtrack in its entirety at New York's Merkin Concert Hall. He wrote the music in 1959 as the score for Jack Gelber's play of that name, a story about heroin-addicted jazz musicians. Redd not only composed the music, which Blue Note released, he acted in the original stage production in New York, London and Paris, as well as the 1961 film adaptation. He was seventy-eight years old now, and he hadn't publically performed the whole soundtrack in at least a decade.

When *The Connection* debuted at Manhattan's Living Theatre on July 15, 1959, it sent what some described as shockwaves through the American theater community. First, there's the subject matter. The play is about junkies waiting around for their "connection" to deliver drugs. The dealer's name is Cowboy, and like most dealers, he keeps his customers waiting. The entire play takes place in a single, dingy Manhattan apartment, while eight addicts pace and fret and kill time. Some of the men are jazz musicians, and between loose, seemingly improvised riffs about money, happiness, loneliness and need, they play songs. Like windsocks brought to life by a fleeting gust, the musicians rise from whichever surface they're slumped on, play a tune then settle back on their piano or stool. The story's plot is best summarized by the title of saxophonist Tina Brooks' 1961 Blue Note album *The Waiting Game*. In the Aristotelian sense, there's little action. Many modern viewers would complain: "Nothing happens!" But that's what makes *The Connection* such a lifelike document: downtime is not only the addict's curse, it's the primary unit of measure in a musician's life.

As author Sam Stephenson says in his book *The Jazz Loft Project*: "Jazz musicians spend a lot of time waiting. Waiting to get called for gigs, then waiting for the gigs; waiting for a pianist or drummer to show up; waiting for a turn to solo; waiting to get paid by a club or label owner. Bassist Bill Crow said, 'There was a lot of idle time in the afternoons. We learned which museums and galleries were free, and we'd go look at the art in the afternoons, when we weren't practicing.'" Others passed the time getting high or attempting to.

It's no exaggeration to call the Be Bop and Hard bop jazz eras the Heroin Age. What cocaine was to the white collar, urban 1980s, and LSD to the '60s, junk was to jazz between the mid-40s and early-60s. As sick as it sounds, the list of the era's players who used heroin, however briefly, reads as the ultimate who's who: Charlie Parker, Miles Davis, Sonny Rollins, Sonny Clark, John Coltrane, Paul Chambers, Art Blakey, Hank Mobley, Jimmy Heath, Jackie McLean, Tina

Brooks, Grant Green, Bobby Timmons, Billy Higgins, Lee Morgan, Dexter Gordon, Tadd Dameron, Sonny Stitt, Chet Baker, Art Pepper, Stan Getz, Stan Levey, Fats Navarro, Gene Ammons, Gerry Mulligan and Ike Quebec, not to mention jazz vocalists Billie Holliday and Anita O'Day. It's tempting to treat this all-star lineup as proof of some connection between intoxication and creativity, but it's really only a case of overlapping chronologies: a heroin epidemic struck during a key phase of jazz's development.

After WWII, dope was everywhere, plentiful and cheap. Veterans returned from war with morphine habits due to injuries. Organized crime reopened supply routes from Turkey and the Far East and funneled heroin into America's black urban neighborhoods, where it decimated communities with a particular fury. Harlem alto saxophonist Jackie McLean, who played a musician in *The Connection* and recorded on the soundtrack, remembers its arrival: "It came on the scene like a tidal wave. I mean, it just appeared after World War II. I began to notice guys in my neighborhood nodding on the corner, you know, and so we all began to find out that this is what—they were nodding because they were taking this thing called 'horse.' We called it 'horse' at that time." McLean was fourteen when the War ended in 1945. Charlie Parker was twenty-five and already addicted. Like so many jazz musicians at the dawn of Bop, Parker's inventive and dexterous playing entranced McLean, and the young musician ended up emulating his idol. "I didn't care if someone said I sounded like him," McLean said. "That's what I wanted to do, and that's all I dreamt of doing. I didn't want to be original. I wanted to play like Charlie Parker." Not only did he and other acolytes copy Parker's playing, they copied his lifestyle. "A lot of guys in my community that idolized and worshipped Charlie Parker began to experiment with this drug," he said, "including myself." McLean spent the late 1940s and most of the '50s using, and only achieved a lasting sobriety in 1964.

In the New York City lofts and clubs where musicians hung out, heroin seems to have moved through their ranks like a cold through a group of friends. Which isn't to suggest that its use was universal. The list of artists who never got wrapped up in it is as impressive as the list of users: Horace Silver, Clifford Brown, Donald Byrd, Benny Golson, Kenny Burrell, Tommy Flanagan, Roy Haynes, Curtis Fuller, Wayne Shorter, Lex Humphries, Wynton Kelly, Freddie Hubbard, Duke Pearson, Horace Parlan, Art Farmer, Milt Jackson, Herbie Hancock, Pepper Adams, Lou Donaldson, Louis Hayes and Freddie Redd. It's only to say that addiction was, along with racist club owners, audiences and police officers, a force that shaped this thriving new music.

As sociologist Charles Winick points out in his study "The Use of Drugs by Jazz Musicians," 16% of the 357 New York jazz musicians he interviewed in 1954 and 1955 were junkies. Winick estimated the total number of working jazz musicians in the City at 5,000, which means that over 750 of them were regular heroin users. In his book *Coltrane: The Story of a Sound*, *New York Times* jazz critic Ben Ratliff acknowledges the scourge but insists we greet Winick's study with caution. "[C]onsider what subterfuges a jazz musician might have been using with a clipboard-holding member of the straight world," says Ratfliff, "and what kind of personality would have submitted to such an interview in the first place." There's another problem.

Discussing drug use can easily draw too much attention to the making of music and the celebrity behind it, and away from the thing that matters most: the music. Do you like it? Does it move you? Or worse: it can appear to glorify drugs. Yet for better or worse, jazz and heroin will always be connected, in the same way that brilliance is sometimes connected to madness, and brilliance connected to intoxication, which connects brilliance to madness to self-medication in misleading cultural archetypes.

The Connection deals with none of that. The play isn't a polemic. It doesn't make a case for or against anything. It isn't a critique of what cats in the Beat Generation would've called "straight society." Rather, as theater critic Kenneth Tynan says in his introduction to Grove Press' published version of the play: "'The Connection' offers no answers; it simply states the problem, and implies the questions." The main question being: aren't we all looking for a fix? Whether through drugs or romance, eating or shopping, the search for satisfaction lies at the heart of the human condition, or as Tynan puts it: "The junkie seeks euphoria. The average citizen seeks happiness. How do these goals essentially differ?" The difference is that, in our pursuit of happiness, some of us seek pleasure or escape, while others seek enlightenment and release from further desire. The far gaze of history suggests which types of seekers Charlie Parker and John Coltrane were. Coltrane gave up drugs and drinking in 1957 and sought spirituality through music. As Parker once told his wife about his failure to quit using: "You know, you can get it out of your body, but you can't get it out of your brain."

In addition to its subject matter, *The Connection*'s format unsettled many viewers. Gelber and director Judith Malina wanted the production to feel more like life than theater. In order to create a sense of realism, Gelber employed a metafictional structure long before the term 'metafictional' existed. Then described as "a play-within-a-play," one of the story's conceits is the idea that the men on stage aren't actors, but real addicts. The performance opens with a man named Jim Dunn addressing the audience. He introduces himself as the play's producer, and the man next to him, Jaybird, as its author, and he describes how the heroin addicts on stage were selected "to improvise on Jaybird's themes." "I can assure you," Dunn says, "that this play does not have a housewife who will call the police and say, 'Would you please come quickly to the [name of theatre].

My husband is a junkie.'" Without warning, the house lights go on and Dunn says, "Please turn the house lights down," further blurring the line between fiction and reality.

One of the "actors," the bass player, asks, "Hey, Jim, is Cowboy back?"

Dunn says, "No, man, Cowboy is not back."

Soon after, Dunn tells the audience, "Our other actors are off in the real world procuring heroin."

Leach, whose apartment the play is set in, corrects him: "Actors?"

Dunn says, "All right, junkies."

Such an approach seems passé to us now. Living as we do in a world where people on homemade YouTube videos can earn five minutes of fame, and reality TV stars can ham for the cameras while their shows maintain the "reality TV" label, we're too savvy about the nature of manufactured truth. But in 1959, Malina and Gelber's cutting edge methods were convincing. The fact that Freddie Redd, Jackie McLean and the two other musician characters actually played their instruments bolstered Dunn's claim that the event was not staged. And although the audience likely didn't know it, McLean grasped the nuances of his role from first-hand experience. He'd spent the last thirteen years using heroin and had only gotten clean that year. The irony of a recovering addict playing an addicted saxophonist must not have been lost on anyone who knew him. Surely the irony of his last name hadn't escaped his friends, either. "Mah-*clean*?" I imagine people saying. "Yeah right." But his role reflects the production's Russian dolls design: actors playing non-actors; real musicians acting as real musicians; an addict playing an addict.

To further add to the illusion, *The Connection* broke down the barrier between audience and actor. The troupe's cofounders ascribed to French playwright Antonin Artaud's idea that theater should dissolve the so-called fourth wall to expand the audience's role beyond that of spectators, and should shock them out of complacency. To do this, the musicians addressed the audience during the show. They hung out on stage as theatergoers arrived, and they panhandled in the auditorium during intermission. Can you imagine, actors hitting you up for money between sets? That alone must have convinced even the savviest attendees. Then, during the second act, a man planted in the audience stood up and interrupted the performance with some dialogue. (Although uncredited in the New York production's program, that plant was Martin Sheen.)

As Gelber's friend, the playwright Edward Albee, said: "I was so affected and energized by 'The Connection'… It was exciting, dangerous, instructive and terrifying, all things theater should be." A number of critics praised it. In the *New Republic*, Robert Brustein described it as "the only honest and balanced work ever created by a Beat Generation writer." Harold Clurman in *The Nation* recognized it as a timely cultural document: "It is as if one had looked for a moment into a corner of our city to breathe the rank air of its unacknowledged dejection. The play reeks of human beings." And Henry Hewes in *The Saturday Review* said: "In its stubborn insistence upon being what it is, THE CONNECTION emerges as the most original piece of new American playwriting in a long, long time."

But many dailies panned it. *The New York Times'* drama critic Louis Calta dismissed it as "a farrago of dirt, small-time philosophy, empty talk and extended runs of 'cool music.'" As Gelber told *The New Yorker* in 1960, "At first, we thought the play would close." A year after opening, though, some fifteen thousand people had seen it. But if some viewers found its subject or construction flimsy, the play's technical ramifications worried others. As John H. Houchin says in his book *Censorship of the American Theatre in the Twentieth Century*, these critics "equated the improvisational informality with an attack on art." Houchin quotes critic Walter Kerr to illustrate this fear about the end of "traditionally crafted" plays. "There is a serious and genuine undercurrent running beneath the styles and anti-styles of our time," Kerr says, "an undercurrent that honestly distrusts art as art, a conviction that whatever is organized must therefore be falsified. It has led not only in experimental drama but in other media as well—to a notion that truth is never to be found in meditation, and certainly not in premeditation, but only in what pops out on the spur of the moment, only in what is wholly or at least partially improvised."

What Kerr misses is the fact that *The Connection* functioned as a de facto document of a passing moment in jazz—another metafictional twist. The play captured real life, and in order to do so, tried to blur the boundary between drama and real life, which some feared undermined the credibility of theater itself, even though all life is theater, and theater is, by nature, like literature, drama manufactured to recreate real life in a highly distilled form more lifelike than that which it reflects. How much more meta can you get? Between its story and construction and Kerr's critique, *The Connection* is Pirandellian. It shows how art and artifice mix, how reality is both true and false and, like the art that attempts to represent it, simultaneously accurate and unreliable.

•

The connection between drug use, creativity and psychological instability presents a chicken-or-the-egg conundrum: do creative people become drug users more frequently than non-creatives? Do artists use drugs because they're psychologically unstable or to try to enhance their creativity? Or is it because so many artists are, by nature, risk-takers? Or subversive? Or trying to maintain the euphoria of the creative act once it's over? The most unsettling question is the furthest reaching: do drugs help make creative people more or less creative?

It's no secret that drugs destroy people. History is filled with examples of talented artists whose careers were derailed, or lives ended, by even casual heroin use. Jimi Hendrix, Janis Joplin and Billie Holiday come to mind. The essential truth of sustained drug dependence is that it consumes the dependent, and it reduces the quality and/or volume of their creative output. But closer inspection of the famously addicted reveals not exceptions to the rule so much as nuances within the usual progress of things. Namely: despite its withering effects, the opium poppy's pungent tar doesn't necessarily prohibit all creativity in the early stages of use. Sometimes talented addicts create powerful lasting works despite themselves, although these artists were talented and at least a little disciplined to begin with.

I hate to say that, but it's true.

Take, for example, pianist Sonny Clark. He was one of the most in-demand sidemen at Blue Note Records, with a seductive style and a legendary sense of rhythm that, according to saxophonist Johnny Griffin, "used Bud's [Powell] basis for power and attack on the piano, but he had another finesse and an exceptional technique, too." He also had a serious narcotics problem. His first record for Blue Note, *Cool Struttin'*, is hailed as essential Hard bop, a model of the bluesy, gospel-infused style that grew out of, and was a response to, Bop. But the bulk of Clark's recorded output ranks as some of jazz's best. Listen to the delicacy of his playing at the 3:24 mark in "I Cover the Waterfront" on *Standards*—the elegance, soft touch, each note confident and deliberate. Listen to his piano part on "Deep Night." That solo isn't only one of the highlights of *Cool Struttin'*, it's one of the most stirring performances in Hard bop. Listen to the piano part on Tina Brooks' song "Minor Move." Technically, the solo is flawed, yet the emotion that pervades it is potent. There's such urgency there, a darkness, and searching. I lack the vocabulary to better express the qualities I hear in any of these examples, but the feelings they elicit are so strong that every repeated listening reminds me that feeling is the reason I listen to music at all. How do you describe a feeling or a musician's style? Clark once tried: "Your soul is your conception, and you begin to have it in your playing when the way you strike a note, the sound you get and your phrasing come out of you yourself, and no one else." But Clark's soul was troubled.

Clark shot a strong dose one night at W. Eugene Smith's loft in Manhattan, leaving him slumped on the ground, muttering and lapsing in and out of consciousness. His friend Lal Halliday, a fellow addict, sat beside him, and as he struggled to keep Clark upright and awake, Halliday told the loft's owner, "Look at this cat. You know, he's one of the best piano players alive and he's killing himself." Clark had overdosed in a stairwell in that very apartment building the previous month; Halliday's seventeen-year old, pregnant girlfriend resuscitated him. Clark recorded his last session as a leader, *Leapin' and Lopin'*, three months later. Depending on who you ask, *Leapin' and Lopin'* is either the worst album in his small catalog, or one of his best. Regardless of one's opinion, one thing is for sure: a teenager's CPR changed jazz history. Thanks to her, Clark lived to play on Dexter Gordon's definitive *Go!*, Jackie McLean's *Tippin' the Scales*, and Clark's legendary quartet sessions with guitarist Grant Green. A year and a half after his overdose, Clark played a show in Junior's Bar at the Alvin Hotel on Fifty-Second Street and Broadway, across the street from Birdland, and died of an overdose afterward. It was the same hotel where Lester Young spent his final days. Clark was thirty-one years old.

There are others.

In 1954, saxophonist Sonny Rollins, considered one of the 1950s' leading tenor players, recorded three originals for a Miles Davis album that became jazz standards: "Airegin," "Doxy" and "Oleo." That same year, he left New York City to kick heroin.

Take pianist Elmo Hope. He wrote searing compositions such as "Bellarosa" and "Weeja" before losing his cabaret card for a drug arrest. In 1957 he moved to LA so he could earn a living performing. When he returned to New York in 1961, he was imprisoned for drug possession and later died of a heart attack at age forty-three.

Take the tenor player Tina Brooks. Brooks wrote one of the undisputed masterpieces of Hard bop, the song "Street Singer." In the span of three years, he recorded four albums as a leader for Blue Note, yet after 1962, he never recorded again. Heroin addiction, jail time and stints in the hospital reduced his activity. Brooks died in 1974, at forty-two.

Charlie Parker might be the most obvious example of a musician who briefly thrived despite himself. During what could be called the mid-career of his lifelong heroin dependence, Parker, sometimes solo, sometimes with his band mates Dizzy Gillespie and Miles Davis, wrote the songs that defined Be Bop: "Confirmation," "Billie's Bounce," "Now's the Time," "Ko-Ko," "Anthropology" and "Scrapple from the Apple." Mostly, though, the opposite is true: jazz's best-known mid-century masterpieces were recorded *after* their musicians sobered up, often only months after.

Following years of addiction and time behind bars throughout the '50s, Dexter Gordon kicked heroin and immediately recorded what are considered his greatest works: *Doin' Alright* and *Go!*.

After his year away, Sonny Rollins returned to New York and recorded not only classic sides with the Max Roach-Clifford Brown Quintet, but his own masterpieces, *Saxophone Colossus* and *A Night at the Village Vanguard*.

Drug problems plagued Miles Davis from 1950 to

1954, but when he finally cleaned up and started taking songwriting and arranging seriously, he spent the next five years recording some of the most popular albums in jazz: his Gill Evans collaborations *Miles Ahead* and *Sketches of Spain*, his classic Quintet sessions *Workin'*, *Steamin'*, *Cookin'* and *Relaxin'*, and his modal masterpiece, the best-selling jazz album of all time, *Kind of Blue*. Davis's sax player John Coltrane experienced a similar trajectory.

Coltrane descended into heroin addiction early in his career. Dizzy Gillespie fired him in 1951 because of drug problems. Singer Johnny Hodges fired him in 1954. Then Davis asked him to join his new quintet in the summer of '54. Sonny Rollins was Davis' first choice, but Rollins was busy kicking his own habit and didn't feel ready. The band recorded their first record together, *'Round About Midnight*, in 1955, but Coltrane was still using. In mid-April, 1956, Davis fired him for showing up to shows drunk and high and more disheveled than the well-tailored Miles insisted his band look; he hired Rollins to replace him. This marked the end of Davis' First Quintet, often hailed as one of jazz's most potent pairings of musicians.

Coltrane realized his addictions were impairing his ability to develop as a player and make the musical statements he wanted to make. In May of 1957, he locked himself in a room at his mother's house in Philly, with only cigarettes and water, and kicked heroin cold turkey. He quit drinking alcohol, too. On May 31st, he recorded his first album as a leader, entitled *Coltrane*. The song "Straight Street" announces the new attitude that would ultimately guide him for the rest of his life. The album also marks the beginning of a career spent changing the face of music. Four months after *Coltrane*, at age thirty, he recorded one of jazz's most celebrated albums, *Blue Train*. It went gold. After Davis rehired him in 1958, the band recorded *Kind of Blue*, and Coltrane followed that with his own *Giant Steps*, an iconic, must-have album which opened up a world of sonic possibilities.

In addition to his new clarity, Coltrane became intensely disciplined. He practiced obsessively and, free of the twin burdens of sedation and the waiting game, could now concentrate wholly on his development. You can hear the effects on the records. Compare Coltrane's strong but uneven solos on "Ah-Leu-Cha" on Davis' *'Round About Midnight*, and "If I Were a Bell" on *Relaxin'*, with his solos on "Time Was" and "Bakai" on *Coltrane*. Amid the hesitations and discontinuous ideas in the former, there are many incredible moments, but the latter solos are continuous, precise, otherworldly exhibitions of brilliance. It's during this newly sober period that Coltrane began perfecting a unique style that jazz critic Ira Gitler described, in October 1958, as "sheets of sound." Jazz, like Coltrane, would never be the same again.

If there's a lesson from the history of Bop and Hard bop, it's this: even though you might thrive briefly while using, you're going to write more and better material sober. Practice and discipline produce the best art, not intoxication. Phrased so simply, the truth of it sounds trite, but in our world of temptation and ambition, where every year rock and pop stars fulfill the familiar arc of the addict-cliché, and too many aspiring artists search for shortcuts to greatness, jazz's truth always bears repeating.

Consider the practical ramifications of a day in the life of Charlie Parker. As his drummer Stan Levey describes it: "He would play all night in the club. Then you'd go up to Minton's [Playhouse in Harlem] at nine in the morning or whatever and play there till about noon. Then you'd have to get more drugs. If you could get a few hours' sleep in between it would be okay, but then you had to get the *money* for the drugs. It was a constant murder. Twenty-four hours a day. Hocking things. Finding money. Getting guys to help you with money. Total waste of time. Complete waste of time. If he had put that time into his music, into his writing, think what would've come out of it, you know?"

In many ways, the characters in *The Connection* give us a glimpse into the daily lives of brilliant composers such as Elmo Hope, Sonny Clark and Tina Brooks and reveal how, off the bandstand, they resembled leaky radiators, dissipating heat and wasting energy. Besides its soundtrack, this is the lasting achievement of *The Connection*: not only as a successful experiment in provocative, improvisational theater, but as a visceral portrait of all that jazz achieved despite its shortcomings. The play's seeming lack of drama, and the glacial pace where nothing appears to happen, impresses upon the viewer the experience of time squandered, potential unrealized. If nothing "happens" in *The Connection*, it's because the play is forcing you to think about how much more *could have* happened had these people—or even us, in our own lives—not spent so much of their waking lives waiting and numbed.

On March 12, 1955, Parker died at age thirty-four, in front of the TV. The official cause of death was pneumonia and advanced cirrhosis of the liver, and he might have also had a heart attack. The specifics are irrelevant. He was in such bad shape in general that the coroner mistakenly guessed Parker's age to be between fifty and sixty. Jazz offers a conflicted legacy, but in the end, a triumph: look at the body of work, the feeling and beauty and lasting effect of a canon created between these creative and consumptive poles. Sobriety and oblivion. Production and obliteration. Coltrane and Parker. Wynton Marsalis captures this complex truth best when he says, "[Jazz] says, 'This is.' And that's it: this is. It deals with the present. Yes, all of that is what happens. Somebody was laying out drunk in the street. It might've been the cat who's playin'. It might've been Charlie Parker. But that fact doesn't alter the power—that *is* the power of what he's saying: yes, I did that, and I also do this. It's the range of humanity that's in this music."

Parker's death devastated his friends and fans. People painted the words "Bird Lives" on walls throughout Greenwich Village. As Jackie McLean remembered: "I didn't go to his funeral. I just couldn't go. I couldn't be a part of that." But he already was.

In the proceeding four years, McLean continued to use drugs and ape the Bop style of his mentor. He'd lost his cabaret card after a narcotics bust and, unable to perform in clubs that served alcohol, earned his money recording. But in 1959, after releasing good but inconsistent albums on Prestige in the mid-50s, McLean sobered up. He signed with Blue Note and recorded *New Soil*, his debut as leader for the label. His friend, the pianist Freddie Redd, connected him with The Living Theatre. And, without knowing it, he started following Coltrane's lead instead of Parker's.

Thinking about it now, or watching *The Connection*'s 1961 film adaptation, it's hard not to wonder: if the play was uncomfortably real for some viewers, how did it feel to McLean? Injecting drugs, waiting for dealers, needles and spoons—many modern addiction counselors would probably say it was unhealthy for people in the early stages of recovery to be around that day to day. Looking back, it's all part of the play's Pirandellian cubism.

Despite its polarized reception, *The Connection* won three Obie Awards in the 1959/1960 season: Best Production, for Judith Malina's direction, Best New Play, for Gelber's script, and Best Actor, for Warren Finnerty's performance as Leach. (Finnerty ended up acting in the film adaptation, too, and bears a striking resemblance to actor Steve Buscemi.) The play became the Theatre's first great success and, for a while, its signature piece, its reputation spread by word of mouth as much as mixed reviews.

Were McLean alive in 2007, he likely would've filled his former spot in Redd's quartet at Merkin Hall. He'd been teaching for years at the Hartt School of Music at the University of Hartford, Connecticut but had recently fallen ill and quit performing. He died in March, 2006, less than twelve months before Redd's re-Connection.

•

The 2007 concert was part of Merkin Hall's "Re-issue: Classic Recordings Live" series. Other performances in the series included Andrew Hill's lost-for-thirty-four years *Passing Ships*, Miles Davis' influential *Bitches Brew*, and a tribute to cornetist Don Cherry. The venue advertised the event as a "comeback story," and Redd as a "forgotten Be Bop pianist" who was reemerging "from obscurity." Although this characterization was the sort of hyperbolic description designed to grab peoples' attention, and even though Redd wasn't technically a Be Bop pianist, it did contain some truth. Many jazz fans considered Redd an underappreciated talent. And the gig was Redd's first on the East Coast in nobody-knew-how-long. Even though he'd recorded a few albums since the '60s, he lived in LA and performed far less frequently than he would have liked.

Apparently, in recent years, he'd gotten down on his luck. Money was tight. Some people said he was broke. One fan using the screen name Veteran Groover on the Organissimo jazz message board reported passing conversations he'd had in LA with and about the pianist. Redd was "barely scraping by," said Veteran Groover. He suffered from carpal tunnel and arthritis, couldn't play for more than a few minutes without his hands hurting, and was possibly too broke to buy the medication that eased the pain long enough to perform entire concerts. Redd couldn't even afford first/last month deposit on an apartment, so he'd been living in motels. "I used to run into him over at Atomic Records once in a while, but not lately," said Groover. Redd had apparently played a number of shows in Los Angeles between 2005 and 2006 and then disappeared. "The guy who booked him into Metropol (a great little club near downtown LA) says he can't find him anywhere," Groover said. "Too bad, as he had a standing offer to play there once or twice a month." Groover also reported that he'd attended some of those Metropol shows and, while some were topnotch, Redd struggled during others.

As tempting as it is to do otherwise, it's best to treat an anonymous poster's info with a grain of salt. Whether or not any of Groover's info was true, even Redd was aware of his reputation for being elusive. "If you're not working in venues where people know where you are, then you're underground," Redd said in the liner notes of his 1991 album *Everybody Loves a Winner*. "It wasn't something that I planned."

I attended the 2007 Merkin Hall show. The 450-seat venue was nearly sold out, the program divided into three parts. First, saxophonist Lou Donaldson performed a short, introductory set. Eighty-one years old, Donaldson came up during the Be Bop years playing with Milt Jackson, Thelonious Monk and Elmo Hope, and he worked his age into numerous Viagra jokes at Merkin. Before playing "Bye Bye Blackbird," he dedicated the song to the man who made it popular, Miles Davis, "when he still played jazz." The crowd erupted in laughter, and Donaldson blew his horn.

Between sets, WGBH radio host Steven Schwartz interviewed Redd on stage, asking about his career, his approach to music, and the history of *The Connection*. The most shocking revelation: that Redd hadn't owned a piano to practice or compose on for decades. The Kaufman Center later presented him with a Korg 01/WFD synthesizer to take home. Maybe Veteran Groover was right. Maybe Redd was struggling financially.

Then came the main attraction: Redd's quartet doing *The Music from "The Connection."* Saxophonist Donald Harrison filled McLean's spot. Veteran Mickey Bass played bass. The legendary Louis Hayes played drums. Among other things, Hayes played on many of Horace Silver's best early albums and, my favorite of all, played on Coltrane's cover of Billy Strayhorn's haunting "Lush Life." The middle section of that song, where Coltrane fades out and lets Hayes' soft brushes do figure eights under Red Garland's blue twinkling piano, is some of the most beautiful music ever recorded.

When the musicians walked on stage, applause filled the hall. People hooted. They cheered. Much of the audience stood in ovation as the players took their places. Redd wore a light yellow sport coat over a blue shirt, his eyes hidden in the shadow of his signature broad-brimmed hat. But there was no missing that smile. It stretched across his face, a bright white crescent in the orange-colored room.

The band tore through the soundtrack in the order it appeared on the album: "Who Killed Cock Robin," "Wigglin,'" "Music Forever," "Time To Smile," "Theme For Sister-Salvation" and "Jim Dunn's Dilema." Even though all the songs are solid, the closer, "O.D.," is the highlight. It starts with a dark pounding piano chord. Boom, boom, boom—played at the rate of a beating heart. First, its frequency resembles anticipation. At this point in the play, the song accompanies the scene where Cowboy, the dealer, hands Leach more dope. Leach is excited, anxious to get it in his vein. Then Leach's anticipation turns to terror when he OD's and crumples onto the table. Here

Redd's pounding keys become both the desperate pumps of a straining heart and a nervous audience waiting. Boom, boom, boom. Will Leach survive? Boom, boom, boom. Will this heart quit beating? "O.D." is a brilliant pairing of sound and scene, though you don't need the play to feel the song's intensity.

During a quiet moment between songs, Redd told the crowd that he might not have enough money to get back to LA, and may need to take up collection for airfare. Laughter spread through the hall, but it felt more nervous than humored: was he serious? Can that be true? People didn't seem to know what to think. Such a talented composer, able to draw this big a crowd, broke? Maybe he was being self-effacing, humbling himself in the face of his enthusiastic reception, but some of what Veteran Groover said might also have been correct.

During one song, Mickey Bass suddenly set down his bass and walked off stage. Audience members glanced at each other, confused, yet the musicians didn't flinch. What was going on? Before anyone could say a word, a young man jumped on stage, lifted Mickey's bass and eased right into the tune. It turns out that Bass's hand had seized up, and the guy who saved the day was Donald Harrison's bass player, Dwayne Burno. Bruno knew Redd's tunes from playing them with Harrison. As a trumpeter in the lobby later told me while discussing that moment: "It's no fun getting old." Age was one theme of the night.

Redd, Hayes, Donaldson—these giants had outlived most of their associates. Booker Little died at twenty-three. Clifford Brown at twenty-five. Bobby Timmons: thirty-eight. Wynton Kelly: thirty-nine. John Coltrane: forty. Grant Green forty-three. By those standards, Hank Mobley seems ancient when he died at fifty-five. Yet here was Poppa Lou Donaldson. And somewhere in New Jersey, was Donald Byrd, age seventy-eight. And Horace Silver in California. And in and around New York City, Curtis Fuller, Jimmy Heath, Paul Cranshaw, Roy Haynes, Sonny Rollins and Jimmy Cobb. And here I was at Merkin Hall, feeling connected to them all beyond time and space, and feeling connected to the strangers in neighboring seats, by the force of this powerful music. As essayist Gerald Early says, jazz is uniquely able to capture the loneliness in the human condition. The fact that "no matter how much you yearn for community, in the end," says Early, "there is this loneliness, and there's no way you can escape it. And that's, to me, what the best jazz, when you hear a soloist, often—especially in a slow piece, or a ballad piece—that's sort of what the best jazz, to me, has always felt like." Yet, as a communal event, a concert can transcend even that fundamental isolation.

After the show, a crowd gathered on Redd's side of the stage. People shook his hand, set roses on the stage, and offered a passing "Freddie!" as they walked by. He smiled and waved back, his eyes hidden under that hat. I slipped among the throng as Redd talked to fans about what sounded like some obscure facet of his recording history. While he talked, a small group of Japanese fans snapped his photo and handed him Blue Note LPs to autograph. Behind them middle aged men waited their turn, LPs clutched to their chests.

I wanted Redd to sign my ticket stub, but the crowd was too big. I went to center stage and said hello to Louis Hayes. He stood alone by his drum set, sliding his sticks into a small bag. Why was no one talking to him? He'd played on more classic jazz albums than everyone else on that stage combined.

"Mister Hayes," I said. "It was great finally getting to hear you play live."

He came over and shook my hand. "Hey, man," he said. "Thanks for coming out." A large circular green stone hung from his neck, swinging on a chain as he leaned down to talk. I couldn't believe it. One of my two favorite drummers, tied for first with Philly Joe Jones, and he was standing right in front of me. When I asked if he had any other upcoming shows, he said he played regularly with his group the Cannonball Legacy Band. "Adderly," he said, "keeping the flame. But I gotta get home early because my wife will kill me if I stay out too late." We laughed and I said I'd see him soon at one of his other shows. Only as I walked down the aisle did I realize I'd forgotten to get him to sign my ticket.

A crowd filled the lobby, lingering and chatting. I found Lou Donaldson standing by a column, talking with a small gray-haired woman, looking bored. "Hi Mister Donaldson," I said. "Would you sign something for me?"

In a scratchy voice he said, "You got it." He was short, dressed in a crisp, gray, pinstriped suit, and he reeked of cigarettes. He leaned my ticket against the column and asked what name to sign. "Where you from?" When I told him Arizona originally, he smiled and said, "Oh yeah? I'm thinking about moving there."

"Tired of this winter weather?" I said.

He patted his chest. "My lungs." He handed me my ticket, the scent of cigarettes swirling around us.

•

Four years later, on the opposite coast, I saw Louis Hayes play again. This time he was leading a group of young local players in Portland, Oregon. I was excited. In the intervening years, I'd told every jazz fan I knew about that Merkin Hall show, labored to express the thrill of seeing Hayes' eyes close and shoulders sway while doing the sort of fine brushwork you hear on Coltrane's "Lush Life," of watching the way he tapped his sticks to the high hat stand as part of the rhythm. "I've never seen anything like it," I kept saying. Yet I hadn't taken a single photo of him playing. Part of me feared he'd retire or quit touring before

I got see him again. I feared that about all the legendary players. This time I brought my camera, and a vinyl copy of Coltrane's *Lush Life* for him to sign.

Before the show, I stepped into the men's room. I'd attended enough concerts to know that I didn't want anything to distract me, be it a text message or a full bladder. When I stepped to one of the urinals, a door opened and Louis Hayes stepped in. He took the neighboring urinal, behind a small divider. As our streams splashed against the porcelain, he tapped his left foot. Dark leather shoes— tap, tap, tap. I figured this was my big chance to talk to him, the man who Horace Silver brought to New York in 1956 just to play with his quartet, the man who drummed on one of Sonny Clark and Grant Green's blazing quartet collaborations.

I washed my hands. As he stepped beside me to look in the mirror, I said, "Hi Mister Hayes. Nice to have you in town."

He leaned toward the neighboring sink. "It's good to be back." He held up one fist—offering a friendly music-power fist pump—and said, "We're gonna swing it tonight, man." Even at seventy-four, his skin had the healthy glow of a forty year old.

"I saw you play in New York in 2007," I said, "with Freddie Redd, doing the whole *Connection* soundtrack."

He stared at me hard, thinking. With one eye squinted and the other wide, he glanced at the ground, then he looked back up, staring at me over the tip of his nose. "Freddie Redd?" he said. "*The Connection*? Nah. I didn't play no *Connection*, man." He sunk his crumpled paper towel in the trash without even looking, and snickered in a tone that said, *You dummy.*

Choosing words that sounded both polite and clear, I smiled and said, "Well, I was there, Mister Hayes. I remember you playing the drums very clearly."

He shook his head, smirking and glancing around the bathroom. "*The Connection*," he said. "No. Wasn't me."

I laughed. "I was definitely there. I even talked to you after."

He said, "You were there?"

"Yeah, I was there. It was one of the highlights of my musical life." I thought of the joke he's made about getting home early to please his wife, but I didn't mention it.

He tested the buttons on his white collared shirt. "Okay," he said. "Hey, maybe I did." I wondered if this was a sign of age or just the byproduct of playing so many stellar shows for so many years that even the ones that fans build up as mythic and one of a kind are still routine enough to slip his mind.

The sound of a saxophone trilled from the other side of the door—his band mate practicing.

I said, "Would you mind signing a record for me after the show?"

He stepped to the door, gripped the handle and raised

his other hand in another friendly fist pump. "You got it, man. Absolutely. I'll see you then."

Among the Throngs:
The Legacy of Lucky Thompson

If you visited Seattle in the early 1990s, you shared the streets with tons of musicians. Grunge legends like Mudhoney and Nirvana walked alongside Eddie Vedder wannabes and legions of hopefuls writing the hits that never were. Living among them was Lucky Thompson, a jazz saxophonist from mid-century New York.

A pioneering tenor with a soft touch and inventive sensibility, Thompson played with everyone from Count Basie to Louis Armstrong during swing's heyday, and on through the creation of Be Bop and Hard bop. He recorded a number of his own standout albums, such as *Lucky Strikes* and *Lucky Thompson Plays Happy Days Are Here Again*, though not as many as his creativity warranted, and when it came to making history, he was in the right place at the right time both inside and outside of the studio.

Eli "Lucky" Thompson was born in Columbia, South Carolina, in 1923 and honed his chops in Detroit. Talented and driven, Thompson practiced his fingerings on a broom before he could buy his own sax, and right out of high school in 1942, he joined trumpeter Erskine Hawkins's big band. After that, he toured with xylophonist Lionel Hampton in

1943. He recorded with Dinah Washington in 1945 and Thelonious Monk in 1952. When Charlie Parker led his first session for Dial Records in 1946, Lucky played tenor on it, etching himself into history on the now legendary bop standards "A Night in Tunisia," "Ornithology," "Moose the Mooche," and "Yardbird Suite." William P. Gottlieb, taking his famous photos of young Duke Ellington and Miles Davis playing tiny Manhattan clubs like the Three Deuces, photographed Lucky too. Listen to Lucky's solo on Miles's 1954 tunes "Blue 'n' Boogie" and "Walkin'": The man played with feeling and fire. "The way he starts from nothing and builds a solo from a whisper to a scream," said Lucky's friend Kenny Washington, "that tenor-saxophone solo was a big influence on a lot of musicians."

The sessions Thompson did with Charlie Parker are some of jazz's most influential and, according to critic Will Friedwald, contain "virtually all of the foundation blocks of Be Bop." Songs like "Ornithology" and "Yardbird Suite" pushed jazz into new, uncharted directions, where it continued to evolve, and Thompson's playing, as *New York Times* jazz critic Ben Ratliff wrote, connected "the swing era to the more cerebral and complex Be Bop style." Thompson's work on Miles's "Walkin'" and "Blue 'n' Boogie" also bridges styles and eras. With Horace Silver's gospel-infused piano, these songs signaled that a new, more melodic form of jazz, later named Hard bop, was emerging from its speedy labyrinthine predecessor Be Bop. Lucky was at the birth of both.

Whether playing as a sideman or playing in his own band, Thompson was inventive. Before John Coltrane made the soprano sax a jazz instrument on his 1961 hit "My Favorite Things," Thompson had already started experimenting with it in France in 1959. He'd moved to Europe in 1957, frustrated with the booking agents and promoters he called "parasites" and critical of record companies' exploitive practices and royalty systems. Thompson advocated that musicians create their own publishing companies to maintain the rights to their music. Avoid the vultures, he argued, protect your creative capital. Recordings of the experiments he made in France weren't distributed in America until 1999.

Thompons' career moved slowly. He grew suspicious. To interviewers and friends, he talked of conspiracies; he felt preyed upon. There were musicians, and there were the powers that be, and the powers that be seemed to be getting the sweeter deal.

Thompson had a legitimate beef with the industry; he also suffered from what was either a mental illness or early stage dementia. "He was paranoid," his friend Lola Pedrini told the *Seattle Times*, "and it wasn't just something that happened in later life; he was always saying that people were taping him and that mics were hanging down." Pedrini described Lucky as "a hermit." His mental state complicates the portrait of his genius, but it doesn't undermine his argument about exploitation. "He was a great human being," she said. "He was the most cordial, gracious, articulate, intelligent musician. He just had a paranoid part to him that kept him from being like the rest of the musicians in this world."

Thompson's contempt for those who interfered with him grew. He wasn't the only one. American music is African-American music. People of color created jazz, blues, and hip-hop, nearly all the musical forms the world associates with American originality and style. In the mid-twentieth century, jazz musicians such as Don Byas, Kenny Clarke, and Kenny Drew left exploitive, racially segregated America for accepting, appreciative, better-paying Europe. Some, such as Gigi Gryce, quit music entirely. Even though these musicians had a profound, lasting impact on American music, they faced institutional racism in their own country, and very few were paid fairly for their work or their creativity. Naturally, players like Thompson no longer trusted the record companies that supposedly made them a living through recording and promotion. *A living?* I can imagine them saying: *If this is a living, why are so many creative people still struggling to get by? Where does all the money go?* His points are as true today as they were back then: White executives get rich off the backs of their artists, particularly creative black ones.

As jazz fell out of favor in America during the 1970s, Thompson grew disenchanted and struggled to earn a living; many players did. His wife had died suddenly in 1963, and he wanted to spend more time with his two kids. He led workshops at Yale as one of the University's first Duke Ellington Fellows. He briefly taught at Dartmouth in the mid-seventies but, fed up, he eventually quit the music business entirely. After that his story gets hazy.

Some people think he moved to Oregon or Colorado. Some people heard the cops gave him a beating that worsened his dementia. Though the location or details of the beating aren't known, given the rampant violence police continue to inflict on people of color in America, it's a believable scenario. At some point he traded his saxophone for dental work in Savannah, Georgia, and disappeared, apparently living in the woods on sparsely populated Manitoulin Island in Ontario, Canada. When he surfaced in 1994, it was inside the Columbia City Assisted Living Center in Seattle. His family had lost contact with him for twenty years.

•

When I first visited Seattle in the summer of '94, I spent a lot of time around Pike Place and Pioneer Square. My parents and I were vacationing in the Northwest for the first time, and these were must-see spots.

My dad raised me on Duke Ellington, Count Basie, Louis Armstrong, the very musicians Lucky Thompson played with. Big band and swing were Dad's thing, not bop, so as a kid, jazz became our thing. We listened to it at home. We listened to it on family road trips. Dad and I listened to it when he drove me to school. He knew a lot about music, from technical info about piano playing to the history of players and recording techniques, yet neither of us had heard of Lucky Thompson. Thompson was sleeping downtown when we visited Seattle; he checked into the first assisted living facility a few months later. Maybe we passed him on Pine Street or Union. Maybe he was sitting on a bench as my family strolled by. He could have easily stood in a doorway, drinking a cup of coffee without us noticing. Downtown was filled with homeless men and women dressed in soiled jackets during summer and unlaced shoes in the rain.

Back then, I had long hair and listened to guitar bands like Bad Brains, Mudhoney and Soundgarden. I liked distortion, and I liked it loud. Grunge holy sites like the Moore Theater and Crocodile Cafe fascinated me more than jazz, and as much as I loved visiting the Seattle Space Needle and sharing seafood with my folks at a famous oyster bar, I also wanted to see these music venues where the music history I'd been hearing about was being made. I'd seen the iconic MTV images: Eddie Vedder stage-diving from the balcony at the Moore. Fans dancing onstage next to Kurt Cobain at the Paramount. Characters in the movie *Singles* coming out of the Virginia Inn. We passed the Moore and Paramount theaters on the street but never went inside. Instead, my parents and I spent our time wandering downtown among the summer throngs.

As the sun warmed our skin, Puget Sound cooled it. Stall after stall, we browsed Pike Place's bright displays of fragrant Northwest fruit and flowers. We passed the vendors selling leather belts hand-stamped with images of killer whales and large black ravens. The moist air, the old brick buildings, the snow-capped peaks looming in the green distance—I knew immediately I belonged here. The city's public spaces made the city so inhabitable.

Pike Place and Pioneer Square were open areas with lots of food and tourists. Of the two, Pike was more appealing. It had Victor Steinbrueck Park, a small square of cool grass smack in the center, with wooden benches overlooking Elliott Bay's blue water. Homeless people sat in Steinbrueck among the lunching white tourists. They talked and drank beer, smoked cigarettes on the benches and steered each other's wheelchairs. People occasionally handed them spare change. Others shook their heads no at requests. Many of these homeless residents lived in rent-by-the-day hotels and shelters nearby, while some lived in cardboard shelters they built under bridges and in doorways. As my family nibbled smoked salmon and French pastry on the grass, we shared the same sun in what could have been a postcard. Any one of these people could have been Lucky. I wouldn't have known him if I had run directly into him. Back then, I'd never even heard his name. Even if I had and he'd started telling me his life story, I probably wouldn't have believed him.

When you're young, it's too easy to view your elders dismissively. You see them shuffling around town, hunched over handcarts filled with groceries, or struggling to make the apartment elevator work, and you feel bad for them. Maybe you wonder what their life had been in youth, or try to picture the people they were before their decay. They're at the age you'll never be, until one day you are. But that's later. It's easy to do the same to the homeless. Now in midlife, I know better than to make assumptions. You never know who's who. Some of them escaped East Berlin in the trunk of a car. Some of them saw Hendrix play at Woodstock. The woman sleeping on the bench near your family picnic might be part of your history. The music you're listening to might be hers.

•

When Lucky landed in Seattle, the whims of popular taste had shifted. Sub Pop Records had sold the world on the idea that Seattle was the center of a musical revolution on the scale of London in the sixties. Magazines filled with grunge articles. Clueless news crews fumbled through segments. Flannels sold everywhere from thrift stores to high end department stores, and musicians descended like gulls. Seattle was flush with posers and talent. The secret was out. The new music was here, and it was fuzz pedals and power chords and record companies were throwing big money around to find it. An architect of the old music was there, but few people noticed. Lucky's was mid-century music, transistor radio music, somebody else's music. Among the throngs of tourists, homeless, and opportunists, why would Lucky stand out?

Thompson arrived in Seattle with no car, no sax and no belongings. He started living near Pike Place Market and Pioneer Square right in the historic center of downtown, and also sleeping in thickets in the Beacon Hill neighborhood. The portrait of his Seattle years is patchy, but in 1993, a year before Nirvana played their final shows and Kurt Cobain committed suicide, Lucky Thompson was living on downtown streets. Because he walked everywhere, he was very muscular. He was also alone. His daughter and son didn't know where he was. He once told an interviewer: "When you can walk alone, you'll never be lonely." But that didn't keep him dry in the Northwest winter. Fortunately, a few inquiring locals like drummer Kenny Washington and Lola Pedrini got to know him and figured out who he was. Sometimes people let him stay at their homes. Sometimes he slept in copses of urban trees. When Thompson's old jazz friends came to Seattle to play, he visited them. Of saxophonist Johnny Griffin's show at Jazz Alley in 1993, Ratliff writes, "Mr. Thompson listened, conversed with the musicians, and then departed on foot for the place where he was staying—in a wooded spot in the Beacon Hill neighborhood, more than three miles away." He visited pianist Tommy Flanagan when he performed at Jazz Alley, too; Flanagan had played on a few of Thompson's records. You wonder what these musicians thought or said to their old friend, if they tried to help him or offered their hotel rooms and he refused. "He was a strong but sensitive cat," Washington said. "He was like a gentle bear, and society and the music business, it just took him out."

In 1993 and '94, Lucky Thompson's declining health required a few hospital visits, and his friends eventually got him to check into Columbia City Assisted Living. He later moved into the Washington Center for Comprehensive Rehabilitation, where he spent the rest of his life. According to the liner notes of his posthumous *New York City, 1964-65* CD, he rarely talked about jazz. His dementia had worsened. Visitors "found him bitter and paranoid" and, the notes say, "he usually refused or was unable for medical reasons to be drawn into meaningful discussions of his past experiences and achievements." Somehow, on a good day in 1995, local KCMU-FM DJ Daniel Brecker got him to speak, and Lucky spilled many details about the past, from meeting a young Quincy Jones to getting to know Thelonious Monk. This rare interview proved to be his last.

At the time of the interview, Thompson was frail. Even though his words came quickly, many were unclear, his thoughts drifting between coherence and confusion. The interview isn't the best representation of his intellect, and yet it gives a clear sense of his warm personality, and many of his stories contain moments of insight. About his approach to music he says, "Honesty is the key to it all." His advice for aspiring musicians: "We all have gifts. What are yours? . . . That thing called 'responsibility'—are you afraid of it?" And his body of work: "I couldn't scratch the surface of what I really felt inside." Forty-one years after working with Miles Davis, Thompson speaks about that legendary session:

> Well, you can never know when it's gonna be a unique record or not until after the fact. . . . In fact, when we went to the studio—it was at [engineer Rudy] Van Gelder's house over in Hackensack— we hadn't planned on doing those two [songs]. We had something else, but we couldn't quite get it together. . . . It turned out very decent.

Decent is an understatement. The interviewer calls it "a masterpiece of twentieth century music." But as Lucky said, it was just another session full of excitement and potential, so he played his heart out and then called it a day.

Thompson is one of those exceptional tenors who

jazz fans describe as "overshadowed." Coleman Hawkins, Lester Young, and Ben Webster overshadowed many sax players during the swing era, just as Sonny Rollins, Charlie Parker, and John Coltrane overshadowed others later. But when you listen to Thompson now, he's the one casting the shadow, even if his name doesn't register like the names of those players.

Of the slow songs he played, I have many favorites. "Irresistible You" and "We'll Be Together Again" are blue beauties, but "The Hour of Parting" tops my list. It's on *The Beginning Years* album. It sounds like 1940s New York at night: muted trumpet, mid-tempo. It has the big city nervous system of someone wearing a fedora, smoking a Chesterfield, and enjoying a momentary rest before charging on toward their future. It isn't sad. It's just slow. But in Thompson's hands, slow sounds sadly happy and beautiful. Saxophonist Ben Webster often cried while playing his sorrowfully beautiful ballads. Lester Young's sax was known for tearing peoples' hearts out. On "The Hour of Parting," Lucky does the same as his overpowering predecessors, wringing your heart like you want music to before he fills it back up.

In 1968, Lucky recorded a brief speech for a British jazz symposium that was honoring him but that he couldn't attend. The recording appears on the *Lord, Lord Am I Ever Gonna Know?* CD. Lucky admits to feeling unworthy because "I feel that I have only scratched the surface of what I know that I'm capable of doing." Then he urges listeners to support musicians by buying tickets to their shows. "Until you are sure as to whether or not the idols that you worship are of your own choosing, you are indirectly supporting those who are continuously exploiting our profession and the artist." At this point in his career, Thompson was six years away from quitting music, and he might have been wondering if he would ever get the financial stability and recognition he deserved. If he sounds disgruntled, it's very politely, and he had good reason. His talent wasn't rewarded in the market place. He'd played on one of Miles Davis's early records, for god's sake, and look how Miles had rocketed past him to fame.

In the speech, Lucky's tone is friendly and gracious, just as his friends described, and his wisdom carries the weariness that midlife imparts, along with hints of the spiritual. "So reappraise your values," he says, "and see if *you* can be the one to decide as to whether or not the artist or artists that you are idolizing happen to be of *your* own choice." He closes with a request. It's intended for people both inside and outside of music, and in hindsight it applies to those of us who witness other people's suffering, and who easily assume the worst of the people we ignore on the street: "And until that time, God bless all of you," he says, "and do me one favor, don't forget to love and respect one another."

The Lost Footage of Pianist Sonny Clark

Sonny Clark is the one who got away. He's the face you see in still photos but can't see in motion. A brilliant jazz pianist who was in demand during the 1950s and '60s on both the West and East coasts, the only known footage of him playing came from a 1956 TV show called the *Stars of Jazz*, but the film seems to have been destroyed when ABC recorded over many of its reels in order to save money. Blank tapes cost four hundred dollars. The company erased countless hours of footage this way. No one knows how many, but one source estimates that they erased around 130 of the 170 episodes. Clark's was episode #11. The *Stars of Jazz* ran from July 1956 to January 1959 and featured performances from such jazz giants as Art Blakey, Art Pepper, Billie Holliday, Bobby Timmons, Chet Baker, Paul Desmond and Hampton Hawes, making the cultural cost of ABC's cost-saving liquidations immeasurable.

You can hear Sonny tearing up the piano on numerous classic albums like Dexter Gordon's *Go*, Jackie McLean's *Jackie's Bag* and his own masterpiece *Cool Struttin'*. You can hear him playing live on a few concert recordings, like

Oakland 1955 and *Art Pepper...Holiday Flight—Lighthouse 1953*. Unfortunately, you can also hear him OD'ing on heroin in a New York loft in September, 1961. That tape comes from obsessive documentary photographer W. Eugene Smith's apartment building at 821 6th Avenue, whose stairwells and halls Smith rigged with microphones in order to capture the details of daily life. (See Sam Stephenson's fantastic book *The Jazz Loft Project* for photos and details.) The drugs leave Clark moaning on the ground while his friend, a fellow addicted musician, works to keep Clark conscious. As the guy told Eugene Smith, "Look at this cat. You know, he's one of the best piano players alive and he's killing himself." Sonny lived to see another day, and fatally overdosed a year and a half later, during which time he recorded scores of incredible music. But that audio isn't the only animated portrait I want of Sonny. He's one of my favorite musicians, and one of jazz's best, yet he only lives in sound and still images. If you want to see the way Sonny's hands moved and body swayed when he played, if you want to get to know him through his ticks and habits, to see the way he laughed, the way he'd tuck his head while comping or watch him drape himself over his piano between songs, folding his arms in particular ways, you're out of luck. Luck has everything to do with it.

As luck would have it, Clark was in the right place at the right time many times—meeting the right people early on (up-and-coming tenor Wardell Gray), moving to the right cities at the right time (LA and San Francisco) before settling in New York during the fertile era of jazz's post-bop development. There he teamed up with some of the jazz's icons and innovators, from saxophonists Hank Mobley and Sonny Rollins, to Grant Green and Donald Byrd. He recorded on the right record label (Blue Note), and basically served as Blue Note's house pianist during its heyday. Clark was talented. He worked hard. He'd played piano since he was a kid. His hard work paid off, and he got a little lucky. But unlucky when it came to film.

Jazz was so popular between the 1940s and '60s that network TV tried to give the public what they thought they wanted. In his book *Jazz on Film*, Scott Yanow writes: "Jazz musicians have mostly appeared on variety shows or one time specials, but there were a few attempts to have regular series, particularly during the early years of television. Eddie Condon's Floor Show with a half-hour weekly series that aired from January 1949 to June 1950 and featured hot jazz in similar format as Condon's earlier Town Hall radio series. Other pioneering series includes Adventures in Jazz (January - June 1949), Cavalcade of Bands (January 1950 - September 1951), The Hazel Scott Show (July - September 1950), America's Greatest Bands (June - September 1955), which was hosted by Paul Whiteman, and Stage Show (July 1954 - September 1956), the latter featuring Tommy and Jimmy Dorsey as co-leaders with many jazz stars as guests. Music '55 (ten half-hour episodes that aired during July

- September 1955) was hosted by Stan Kenton, and the legendary Nat King Cole Show lasted 59 weeks (September 1956 to December 1957)." As Yanow says, "Typically, many of the televised jazz performances of the 1950s no longer exist." Some televised jazz broadcasts did survive, and you can watch them on YouTube.

On CBS's short-lived *Roy Herridge Theater* series in 1959, Miles and Coltrane play "So What" with their *Kind of Blue* band mates Wynton Kelly and Jimmy Cobb. Art Blakey's classic Jazz Messengers lineup of Bobby Timmons, Lee Morgan and Benny Golson play "Moanin" in 1958. On the *Sound of Jazz* in 1957, Lester Young and his old friend Billie Holiday play together for what was the first time after a long falling out. Cannonball and Nat Adderley play the famous "Work Song" in 1963 with badass drummer Louis Hayes. Sonny Rollins and Jim Hall do "The Bridge" in 1962 in crystal clear footage on *Jazz Casual.* And there's footage of Nina Simone and Grant Green and Bud Powell and Dexter Gordon and Horace Silver. What footage remains is spectacular—a small body of mid-century classics. But for people living in our time of cell phone documentation and a hundred camera angles, the moving record of jazz's great Hard bop era seems paultry and incomplete. (And we don't have any footage of Hank Mobley!)

On Clark's 1956 *Stars of Jazz* appearance, he played with an early iteration of Howard Rumsey's Lighthouse All-Stars, the house band of the famous Lighthouse jazz club in Hermosa Beach, California. The band always consisted of a rotating cast. This incarnation was the first to appear on *Stars of Jazz*, and it featured Howard Rumsey on bass, Charlie Parker and Dizzy Gillespie's drummer Stan Levey on skins, Frank Rosolino on trombone, vocalist June Christy singing, and her husband Bob Cooper on oboe and sax. Transcriptions of the host's monologues survive.

Between songs, he talks about the night's musicians. He talks about their corporate sponsor Schwepp's ("Why don't you try this authentic tonic mixer—the drink made from the magic elixir, with Schweppervesence to last the whole drink through?"), and about West Coast versus East Coast jazz. "From our vantage point here on the Pacific," he says before introducing the next song, "New York seems to have a slightly smug attitude about its position as the cultural center of the Universe. So while the East rests on its provincial attitude, here in the provinces, jazzmen are busy exchanging new ideas, experimenting, and creating fine new music." When the hosts asks the musicians about the benefits of playing in a house band, the saxophonist explains that not touring allows them to have a home life. As for the musical advantages, Clark says: "Working together for long periods of time, we get to know each other well ... which helps our music..." The following year, Clark moved to New York permanently, where he put himself on celluloid and wax over and over again, but never again on film.

Yes, at least we have his music. It's true. And the music always matters more than the story of the artist's life, but music is so intimate that you get to know a player by getting to know their particular sound and style, their signatures, and the same is true of watching their mannerisms and physical habits on their instrument. Some of us want to *know* Sonny more that we do.

Sonny survived childhood in a tiny coal mining town during the racially charged early 20th century. He survived sketchy police stops on dark New Jersey roads to and from recording sessions. He'd survived overdoses and the fickle jazz economy, but with film, his luck ran out. As the Duke Ellington song says, "I guess I'm just a lucky so-and-so." Sometimes yes, sometimes no.

Unapologetic Vision: Miles Davis and the Lesson of 'Sid's Ahead'

On March 4, 1958, Miles Davis' sextet entered Columbia Records' 30th Street Studio in Manhattan. It was their second session for what became the album *Milestones*. The first, in February, had gone smoothly, yielding the bulk of the albums' tracks, including one of John Coltrane's best speeding solos—on "Straight, No Chaser"—and Davis' first modal composition, "Milestones," a song which foreshadowed his album *Kind of Blue* the following year, one of the best-selling albums in jazz history. This second session proved fruitful, yet unbeknownst to them, its turbulence signaled the demise of the band's famous rhythm section, and another major shift in Davis' perpetually evolving musical sensibility.

On that day, the musicians stood by their respective microphones. Red Garland sat at his piano. Before the engineer rolled tape on the song "Sid's Ahead," Davis leaned over Garland's shoulder and fingered the keys to show him something. Nobody knows what exactly was said. Maybe Davis told Red how to play a particular part.

Maybe he criticized his approach to the song. Or maybe he insulted his playing in general. Whatever the specifics, Garland didn't like the critique. Furious, he stood up and stormed out of the studio, leaving Davis with booked session time and no pianist.

It's easy to imagine Davis' possible reactions. You can picture him hurling insults at Red's turned back: "You baby!" You can picture him glancing at his remaining musicians and, in the new silence of Garland's absence, saying, "Oh well, let's play," in that gravely, low voice of his. Or maybe his response was more indifferent, a distant, unaffected call to the engineer—"You ready?"—after which he took his place at the microphone, counted off with four snaps of his fingers, then blew his horn. Davis had a legendary temper compounded by shyness, insecurity, cockiness and sensitivity. It's not unreasonable to imagine him saying something to the effect of "Fuck him, then," and shrugging rather than laughing off Garland's insubordination. After all, it was Miles' band. To save face, he needed to at least maintain the appearance of control.

Whatever Davis' reaction, we know his next move. When the tape started rolling on "Sid's Ahead," he raised the trumpet to his lips and played the song's theme with his two saxophonists. Then he played piano behind their solos. It's an arrangement like no other in his forty-six-year catalog. If you listen closely, you can hear it: there's no piano during the first fifty seconds of the song; there's nothing behind Miles' solo except bass and drums; and there's no piano accompaniment during the first eight or so seconds of Coltrane's sax solo. That eight second pause was likely the time it took Davis to walk from his microphone over to the piano and find his place on the keys.

Spare, haunting in its austerity, Davis' piano playing is competent, his chords effectively maintaining the song's dark mood while giving the soloists propulsion and room to improvise. But the overall result is somehow lacking in what our ears recognize as depth, the song neither on par with the rest from this period, nor second-rate. It's mixed. Yet the band never recorded another full take. Was Davis satisfied with the outcome? Or was he so fed up that he wanted to be done with it? Impossible to say. Even in a career that includes nonets and jazz-rock fusion, the thirteen minute-long "Sid's Ahead" stands out as an anomaly, because it offers an inimitable window into Davis' disposition as a band leader, a role he filled with an erratic, demanding mixture of bellicose pride and determination, foresight and adaptability, and a willingness to change not only with the times, but according to the shifting conditions of his immediate surroundings.

Not long after this session, Davis replaced Garland and drummer Philly Joe Jones with other musicians, and he moved in an entirely new stylistic direction, turning away from the chords that defined Bop and post-Bop jazz—and his and Garland's playing at the time—in favor of the modes and scales immortalized on *Kind of Blue*.

This shift is important historically, but it isn't surprising. Musically, Davis was always changing. "I have to change," he once said. "It's like a curse." It also seemed an extension of his personality. He had a reputation for being mercurial. Novelist James Baldwin captured the trumpeter's essential duality when he characterized him as a "miraculously tough and tender man". The phrase more often used to describe Davis is "Jekyll and Hyde." It illustrates the way his temperament, like his playing, swung between extremes. Cold and heat. Strength and vulnerability. Loud and lyrical. Tenderness and irritability. Bravado and sensitivity. Destruction and creativity. Performance and isolation. His son Gregory even used this convention as the title of a book, *Dark Magus: The Jekyll and Hyde Life of Miles Davis*. In addition to his mercurial nature, Davis had a temper. He yelled at journalists, threatened a few club owners and record executives, hit a concert promoter and also his first wife, Frances Davis. On at least one occasion, he even punched John Coltrane and bassist Paul Chambers. Yet he was as prone to outbursts as he was long silences.

Already shy by nature, complications from a 1955 operation for polyps damaged Davis' vocal chords, producing his signature rasp. Not only did he speak less after the surgery, he become more self-conscious and, according to John Szwed's biography *So What*, "When he did speak, he often was not heard and had to whistle to get attention." This mixture of silence, brooding and unpredictability made him an intimidating presence; it was also part of the reason he was able to direct his band with few if any words.

Accounts vary, but depending on who he was playing with, Davis could be both a reactive and a proactive band leader whose involvement ranged from hands-off to heavy-handed. In a 1979 radio interview, Garland's replacement, pianist Bill Evans, described recording with Davis' new, post-*Milestones* band: "Miles occasionally might say, 'Right here, I want this sound,' and it turns out be a very key thing that changes the whole character of the [song]. For instance, on 'On Green Dolphin Street,' [on the *'58 Sessions* album,] the original changes of the chorus aren't the way [we recorded it]: the vamp changes being a major seventh up a minor third, down a half tone. That was [one when] he leaned over and said, 'I want this here.'"

Drummer Jimmy Cobb, who played with Evans in the new band, remembered Davis being more involved with pianists than with other musicians: "...and piano players, when they first got with the band they were always confused because he [Davis] would tell them when to play and when not to play, so they got so they wouldn't know when to play."

There's a famous story about Davis and Thelonious Monk butting heads during the 1954 session that yielded the albums *Modern Jazz Giants* and *Bags' Groove*. It wasn't

Davis or Monk's idea to play together on this date. Prestige Records label owner Bob Weinstock assembled them and others as an "all-star" group. The results were tense. Rumors about the session circulated afterwards: Davis had argued, cursed and threatened Monk in the studio; he'd insulted Weinstock, asked why, in the words of bassist Charles Mingus, "he had hired such a non-musician" as Monk. One rumor even had Davis punching Monk in the face. The misinformation irritated the trumpeter. In *Miles: The Autobiography*, Davis said, "When I heard stories later saying that me and him was almost about to fight after I had him lay out while I was playing on 'Bags' Groove,' I was shocked, because Monk and I were, first, very close, and second, he was too big and strong for me to even be thinking about fighting [...] All I did was tell him to lay out when I was playing. My asking him to lay out had something to do with music, not friendship. He used to tell cats to lay out himself." As usual, the truth was complex.

First off, Monk screwed up the first take of "The Man I Love." When vibraphonist Milt Jackson played the intro, Monk started in prematurely and asked, "When am I supposed to come in?" You can hear it on *Modern Jazz Giants*. Jackson quits playing. The studio fills with the sound of musicians talking over each other. Irritated, Davis tells studio engineer Rudy Van Gelder, "Hey Rudy, put this on the record, man, all of it." Later, while the band rehearsed "Bags' Groove," Davis told Monk, "During my solo, lay out," meaning, don't play piano behind him, or "comp" as it's called. Davis liked Monk's inventive playing and songwriting; that's why he covered numerous Monk tunes. In the early 1940s, Thelonious had even given Davis lessons about harmony and songwriting, but Davis now had trouble soloing over him. The pianist's comping screwed him up. "I love the way Monk plays and writes," Miles told Nat Hentoff in 1958, "but I can't stand him behind me. He doesn't give you any support." The reason, in Miles' words, was that unlike Red Garland, Herbie Hancock and Bill Evans, Monk didn't play to suit your solo, he "played what he wanted." So Davis told him to lay out.

During "Bags' Groove," Miles sat in a chair, as he normally did, and aimed the bell of the trumpet at the floor. When he started soloing, Monk not only stopped playing, he stood right next to Davis, towering over him. When Miles later asked why he did that, Monk said, "I don't have to sit down to lay out." It seems a passive aggressive move, a Monkish way to voice his displeasure about being told what to do. Back then, jazz musicians also called laying out "strolling," meaning, taking a break or a figurative walk in the interim. According to journalist Ira Gitler, when Monk quit playing during Davis' solo on an earlier take of "Bags' Groove," he ruined the song by asking Van Gelder, "Rudy, where's the bathroom?" If the sources of these snafus sound benign, their subtext was not: Monk didn't like Davis telling him how to play anymore than Davis liked playing over Monk. But as much as it irritated Monk to be directed in this way, in order to play with Monk on this date, Davis had to direct him.

He and Monk quarreled again. After performing at the 1955 Newport Jazz Festival together, the band was riding back to New York from Rhode Island in a limousine, and Monk criticized Miles' playing. He said he played his song "'Round Midnight" incorrectly. "So what?" said Davis. He didn't like the way Monk had comped behind him, and he claimed that Monk was only complaining because he was jealous of the enthusiastic reception Davis received at the festival. Monk, infuriated, flung the door open and stepped out the car, walking to the ferry and riding home by himself.

Bassist Percy Heath recorded with Davis during numerous 1950s dates and was there to witness the tension with Monk in both the studio and at Newport. "Miles liked to accompany people on the piano," Heath said. "He told all his piano players to stroll (not just Monk) and it *was* Miles' record date. Miles always bragged about showing piano players things—he knew how he wanted things to sound." Alto saxophonist Cannonball Adderley had a different experience.

Adderley played with Coltrane, Cobb and Evans on *Kind of Blue*, and also with Garland on *Milestones*. He was in the studio when Red stormed out. Although he seems to agree that Davis "knew how he wanted things to sound," Adderley's impression of Davis' leadership was more nuanced than that of Evans or Heath. "He never told anyone what to play," Adderley said in 1972, "but would say 'Man, you don't need to do that.' Miles really told everybody what NOT to do. I heard him and dug it." In what little studio chatter exists on the *Kind of Blue* master tapes, you can hear what Adderley is talking about. While the band runs through the intro theme for the song "Freddie Freeloader," trying to get it right, Davis stops the take with a whistle and tells pianist Wynton Kelly, "Hey look Wynton, don't play no chord going into the A flat..." Meaning, in this case, Davis was corrective rather than prescriptive, reactive rather than preemptive.

At the beginning of "You're My Everything" on *Relaxin'*, you can hear Davis micro-managing in this way. The tape is rolling. Miles starts running through scales on his trumpet. Chambers hits a few notes on his bass. Then Davis tells the band, "When you see a red light on, everybody's supposed to be quiet." The studio falls silent. Seconds pass. Garland plays the lead to this melancholic ballad in a stream of light, trilling, single notes that resemble his intro to "My Funny Valentine. Then Davis stops him with a snap of the fingers and a piercing whistle. "Play some block chords, Red," Miles says. To the engineer, "Alright Rudy," followed by one more admonishment: "Block chords, Red." Garland begins again, this time leading with a thudding fistful of block chords whose dense edges thicken with sustain, before Davis drizzles his slow, sweet trumpet over them. This exchange took place two years prior to "Sid's Ahead." If it irritated Garland, the tape presents no evidence of it. More importantly, the second, block chord version is more complex and engaging than the preceding intro. Which is to say, Davis' firm direction yielded superior results.

This approach had worked well with other pianists, too, and not everyone minded. About recording "In Your Own Sweet Way" with Davis in 1956, pianist Tommy Flanagan said, "I remember him telling me how to voice the intro. He always knows exactly what he wants. It makes him easy to work with. If you don't play what he wants, he tells you... 'Play block chords, but not like Milt Buckner. In the style of Ahmad Jamal.'" Again, the results are profound.

In his book *So What*, John Szwed further complicates the portrait of Davis the band leader when he describes how Miles retooled drummer Philly Joe Jones' sense of rhythm and timing. "Though Miles seldom told his musicians how to play," says Szwed, "drummers were the exception. He involved himself directly in Jones' playing, telling him not to play a rhythmic figure *with* him but *after* him, or changing the way he played the ride cymbal, the device that carried the basic beat." *So What* is widely considered the authoritative Davis biography, but judging from the above musicians' impressions, Szwed's assertions that "Miles seldom told his musicians how to play" and that "drummers were the exception" ring false. Davis clearly *did* tell numerous musicians how to play, not just drummers, but pianists, many of them seasoned pros. Davis seems to have had no system or consistent method for how he directed who and why; his reactions to different musicians and compositions appear as unpredictable as his varying reactions to fans, promoters, beautiful women and sidemen off the bandstand. About his direction of Jones, Szwed quotes Davis as saying: "And I listen to the top cymbal to hear whether he plays it even or not. He may not play it like I want him to play it, but he can be taught how to play it if he plays even. I changed Joe's top cymbal beat. He was kind of reluctant at first, but I changed it so it could sound more ad lib than straight dang-di-di-dang-di-di-dang: I changed it to dang-di-di-dang-di-di-di-di-dang, and you can play off that with your snare drum." Szwed speculates that "Philly Joe would put up with him messing with the rhythm because Davis himself was such an exceptionally rhythmic player." In a move in keeping with the extremes of his personality, Davis took the opposite tact with his tenor player John Coltrane.

During Coltrane's first stint with Miles between 1955 and '56, the two had a tense relationship. Coltrane was still drinking and using heroin. He was nervous on stage and in the studio, often arrived to shows disheveled, and he was still developing what would forever be known as his sound. During this apprentice period of experimentation and self-doubt, he kept asking Miles for direction. Miles gave him none. In place of answers to what to play and what not to play, Miles gave the opposite of direct guidance: he gave Coltrane so much creative latitude that it put an unspoken pressure on the saxophonist to not only advance musically, but to always be at his best. During live performances, Miles routinely left the stage while Coltrane soloed. And there, alone on stage, as the audience's sole focus, the saxophonist had no choice but to, in the words of jazz critic Ben Ratliff, "strengthen his language." As Ratliff recalls in his book *Coltrane: The Story of a Sound*, a reporter once asked Coltrane if Davis demanded he "play as far out as he could," and Trane replied, "Miles? Tell me something? That's a good one!" That might summarize Davis' entire approach with Coltrane.

As Coltrane said of his experience playing with Davis: "Miles is a strange guy; he doesn't talk much and he rarely discusses music. You always have the impression that he's in a bad mood, and that what concerns others doesn't interest him or move him. It's very difficult, under those conditions, to know exactly what to do, and maybe that's the reason I just ended up doing what I wanted. ...Miles' reactions are completely unpredictable [on the bandstand]: he'll play with us for a few measures, then—you never know when—he'll leave us on our own. And if you ask him something about music, you never know how he's going to take it. You always have to listen carefully to stay in the same mood as he!"

Davis later acknowledged his laissez-faire approach with the tenor, and, in the process, articulated the contradictions between his ideas of leadership and his uneven direction. "I think the reason we didn't get along at first," Miles said, "was because Trane liked to ask all these motherfucking questions back then about what he should or shouldn't play. Man, fuck that shit; to me he was a professional musician and I have always wanted whoever played with me to find their own place in the music. So my silence and evil looks probably turned him off." What it boiled down to was this: Davis had high expectations of his band members, and as willing as he was to tinker, he didn't want his band composed of musicians who needed much guidance.

As drummer Jimmy Cobb speculated, Davis specifically gave Coltrane unusual autonomy because he "sensed that [Coltrane] was working on something." Meaning, he was working on his sound. Davis was drawn to Coltrane's inventive playing from the first time he heard it on a private recording the tenor made when he was nineteen, and he went out of his way to keep him in the band despite Coltrane's initial problems. Because Miles learned to play Bop under the tutelage of Charlie Parker and Dizzy Gillespie, the architects of the form, Miles clearly understood the value of apprenticeship, too.

Whatever the reason for the leeway, the way Davis dealt with Trane was noticeably different than how he dealt with other band members. In retrospect, the differences resemble the well-tailored methodology of the best teachers, where the teacher recognizes that what one student needs at a certain point in their development is different than what another student needs, and that sometimes, as in Coltrane's case, what that student needs aren't guidelines or parameters at all, but freedom, a safe place to explore—as well as the impetus to improve, sober up and behave professionally.

Davis had an ear for talent. In much the same way that drummer Art Blakey's Jazz Messengers functioned as a de facto incubator for budding, young players, so too did some of jazz's best musicians go on to legendary careers after spending time with Miles: Herbie Hancock, Wayne Shorter, Bill Evans, Keith Jarrett, Chick Corea, and of course, Red Garland, Cannonball Adderley, Philly Joe and Coltrane. But being a teacher and providing a proving ground weren't Davis' objectives—making music was—and giving Trane room probably wasn't benevolence on Davis' part. The freedom that Coltrane needed to push stylistic boundaries and develop new ideas also happened to propagate the same fiery, innovative playing that made Davis' music irresistible, and so Davis modified his direction accordingly. The five albums Davis recorded with Coltrane in 1956 inarguably endure as some of jazz's greatest, proof of the effectiveness of his leadership. That, in the end, is the legacy of "Sid's Ahead." That beneath the

Jekyll and Hyde persona, the man so "tough and tender," was an intuitive, impulsive reactionary who, when he wanted a song to sound a certain way, sometimes did as Heath, Cobb, Flanagan and Evans remember and told his musicians what to play, and who, when he wanted a certain sound in other situations, did as Coltrane and Adderley remember and gave his musicians little to no direction at all. He didn't seem to care if his leadership insulted them. He didn't care if they felt neither coddled nor appreciated, smothered or vulnerable. In his mind, he heard the music in a very particular way, and he was determined to bring it to life. As Percy Heath said, it *was* Miles' session after all, and like any good conductor, he conducted his orchestra with few words and numerous gestures.

Despite the contradictory experiences of his sidemen, the portrait of Miles that emerges is one of unapologetic vision. Davis' varying levels of direction was part of his brilliance. It was the force that sculpted what now stands as one of the world's greatest bodies of work. And if it was part of what ultimately ran off Garland, it was also what produced moving results with him and his replacement, Bill Evans, music that millions of people still listen to today, and always will. Even with its skeletal accompaniment and relative flatness, "Sid's Ahead" is a testament to Davis' unwavering devotion to doing things his way and doing them well. It's a way that's hard to take umbrage with when listening to *Milestones* and the rest of his mid- to late-50s albums, even if in making them Miles could be, in Coltrane's words, "a bit of a prick."

Jazz Fiction and Reality:
The Bright Comet of Wardell Gray

By the time one of saxophonist Wardell Gray's most blazing recordings came out in 1956, Gray was dead, his body found on the side of the road outside Las Vegas. He was thirty-four years old.

Gray was one of the West Coast's most talented jazz musicians. Raised in Detroit, Michigan, he settled in Los Angeles in a thriving Be bop scene and played with everyone from Erroll Garner and Billie Holiday to Dexter Gordon and Zoot Sims. Versed in swing and bop, Gray did TV spots. He released his own records and mentored younger musicians like Hampton Hawes and Art Farmer as they established themselves. When Bennie Goodman heard Gray play in 1947, he hired him to join his new modern band. When pioneering bop altoist Charlie Parker recorded a new blues to commemorate his release from Camarillo State Mental Hospital, he had Gray play on it; "Relaxin' at Camarillo" became a jazz standard. Musicians loved Wardell. They loved his sound. He and baritone saxophonist Pepper Adams were close friends, trading novels and watching movies together between gigs, and sharing each other's instruments. "I guess people don't consider there are jazz musicians who are well-read and read for pleasure," Adams remembers. "And I was going to university at the same time, pursuing an English major. Wardell was very interested in what I was doing at college." Gray was playing with Count Basie when he fell in love with his second wife Dorothy A. Duvall. When Gray and Duvall got married in 1951, trumpeter Clark Terry was his witness. Terry nicknamed him "Bones" for his thin, six-foot four-inch frame. When they buried Gray in Michigan four years later, Pepper Adams was a pallbearer.

People have been speculating about Wardell's death since the police closed the case in 1955. The mixture of music and high drama, the lingering mystery of unanswered questions, and the mid-century setting lends itself perfectly to a noir treatment. But this rich material is someone's life we're talking about. Gray was someone's son, someone's husband and father. From the perspective of narrative, though, the questions are too tempting to resist: Who was he? What was he up against? What happened to him?

Best-selling crime novelist James Ellroy mentions Gray's murder in his 2001 novel *The Cold Six Thousand*. Jack Kerouac references Gray in *On the Road*, writing how two Beats, "sandwich in hand, stood bowed and jumping before the big phonograph, listening to a wild bop record I had just bought called 'The Hunt,' with Dexter Gordon and Wardell Gray blowing their tops before a screaming audience that gave the record fantastic frenzied volume."

Author Bill Moody, a jazz drummer himself, turned Gray's story into his 1995 novel *Death of a Tenor Man*. In it, a detective searches for evidence of foul play in a case that cops deemed an open and shut case. Both books are hard-boiled crime stories, and even though they focus on the unfortunate, more tawdry side of jazz and Wardell's life, they do the great service of keeping Gray's name in circulation, so that as jazz music ages and Gray inevitably fades from view, hopefully at least a few people will continue to discover his music. Other writers have turned jazz history into compelling fiction.

Elliott Grennard based his short story "Sparrow's Last Jump" on an infamous 1946 recording session Charlie Parker did for Dial Records. The story appeared in *Harper's* May, 1947. Grennard sat in the session as a correspondent for *Billboard* magazine. Parker came in, struggled with his instrument, struggled to tune up. He played a few legendarily sloppy renditions — including "Lover Man," one of the most poignant, anguished songs he ever recorded, and often considered his worst because he'd drunk a quart of whiskey and been prescribed Phenobarbital — then he left the studio. Ross Russell was such a huge Parker fan that he started Dial Records in order to record Parker. When Russell saw Parker's condition in the studio that day, he said, "I've just lost a thousand bucks tonight." Russell physically propped Parker up during "Lover Man." He also released "Love Man" anyway. The saxophonist never forgave Russell for releasing music made at his lowest, yet despite its flaws, bassist Charles Mingus called "Lover Man" one of his favorite Parker songs "for," in his words, "the feeling he had then and his ability to express that feeling." As scholar Ted Gioia put it in his book *West Coast Jazz,* "The performance is pathetic, but the pathos is gripping: It is a record that few can enjoy, but once put on the turntable it is mesmerizing." I find Parker's playing on it hauntingly beautiful, too, filled with raw emotion that's not simply tortured but reaching, calling out, and charged with a gripping blue agony that's missing in even the most melancholy ballads.

To salvage some studio time, Russell kept the rest of the band playing after Parker left. Out in Los Angeles, Parker powered on. He'd been using heroin for years and often drank heavily when he couldn't score. A mix of drug withdrawals and alcohol abuse, rather than mental instability, sent Parker off the deep end. Twice he staggered into the lobby from his room in the Civic Hotel, naked except for his socks. When he lit his hotel room on fire, likely from falling asleep smoking, the police arrested him for arson and indecent exposure, held him in the Los Angeles County Jail psych ward, then transferred him to Camarillo State Mental Hospital where he spent six months sober, recuperating. He commemorated the experience in his song "Relaxin' at Camarillo," transforming real life into music the way Grennard transformed real life into fiction.

This period was one of the worst in Parker's life. Grennard turned it into literature. Russell turned it into an enduring musical statement. Is that exploitive? Opportunistic? Or is a musical genius's agonizing story worth more to the world than their personal privacy? Parker was one of the world's most influential musicians. People remain fascinated by his brilliance, mystified by his lifestyle, and want more from him than just the music. We want him. It's hard for writers to resist a good story, and maybe the world needs to know what makes brilliant artists tick in order to see what makes us all tick. Although we must pry within reason, peering into people's private lives and interior worlds is what makes literature so rich and engaging.

There are a few good jazz movies based on real themes and history: *Paris Blues*, featuring Sidney Poitier and Paul Newman in 1961, Shirley Clarke's dark underground classic *The Connection* in 1961, and *Round Midnight* in 1986, with sax player Dexter Gordon playing the lead, are the best. Good jazz fiction is harder to come by.

California novelist James Houston tried his hand in 1969. It's called *Gig* and takes place in a coastal California roadhouse. As the dust jacket copy says, it's "the story of one Saturday night around Roy's grand piano, of the people who come to listen and perform, and of the relationship between a performer and his audience." Kazuo Ishiguro published the story collection *Nocturnes*, all built around music, one focused on jazz. One of the most celebrated examples of jazz literature is Michael Ondaatje's novel *Coming Through Slaughter.*

Published in 1976, Ondaatje's book is based on the life of New Orleans cornetist Buddy Bolden. Bolden was a famously inventive player who led an infamous life. In New Orleans, he and "jass" forefathers King Oliver, Louis Armstrong and Bunk Johnson helped shape jazz into the distinct form of music we know it as today. He invented a marching band beat called the "Big Four" which facilitated more improvisation. He played for enthusiastic crowds of people in the streets. Then he disappeared for two years, suddenly reappeared with even stronger musical chops, and at age thirty went what people called "mad" in a parade. He spent the rest of his life in an asylum. None of his recordings survived.

Ondaatje's book is timeless, partly because its humanity, formal experimentation and themes transcend jazz. The author knew a strong protagonist when he saw one, and his fictional Bolden only partially resembles the thin portrait of Bolden historians have. It also rises to an archetype of the wild musical genius, the artist as comet streaking through earthly skies, bright and illuminating, intense and brief, attractive and mystifying, and also confusing. It portrays artists as powerful fragile beings, buckling under our shared mortal pressures while crafting things that live beyond this world and most of our abilities.

For many writers, the historical record isn't the point. They don't need all the answers. They'd rather experiment with the incomplete picture in order to build a new, bigger truth in the space between details.

All of which is to say, readers looking for something compelling to spend time with should consider the small pantheon of jazz fiction. Writers looking to turn real life into dramatic narrative need look no further than the real history of American music. Racism, resistance, creativity, invention, the power to shape global culture while enduring systematic repression, violence, drug use, and the countless personalities with memorable names set against the sprawling canvas of post-WWII New York City, Detroit, Chicago and Los Angeles — it's all there. Hopefully more people will write their own jazz stories. The players are deeply human, talented and flawed, like Parker, Billie Holiday and Wardell Gray.

In 1956, LA's Modern record label released what many consider some of Gray's best music. The recordings were taped live at two concerts in 1947: one on February 27th at Shrine Auditorium in Los Angeles, the other on April 29th at the Civic Auditorium in Pasadena. The songs appear on *Way Out Wardell.* You can hear Gray's inventive mix of swing and bop on "Just You, Just Me" and "Sweet Georgia Brown." They're the kind of solos that might sound standard now, but in the days when new forms of jazz were emerging from big band, these were virtuoso performances that blew peoples' minds. The tired image of the guy with the horn smoking the cigarette on the street corner, the muted trumpet moment on the movie soundtrack — these tropes have inured us to the actual sound of jazz, but stop for a second and listen. Really listen. Solos like Gray's and Parker's are the kind that make the impossible seem casual. They're the skateboarder doing a crazy triple flip on a ramp despite gravity, before we'd seen that a thousand times. They're the first moon landing and the millions of people watching the event on TV from their living room sofas. They're an unscripted feat that pushed the limits of what music could be.

The end of Gray's life goes like this: In 1955, the Benny Carter Orchestra hired him to play on the opening nights of the Moulin Rouge. The Moulin was the first racially integrated hotel-casino in America, and they were going to celebrate with great fanfare. Carter's band played three times a day. Customers flocked to the casino. On the Orchestra's final day, Gray didn't show up to one performance. He missed the late night performance, too. No one knew what was up. The following day, a stranger found him with a broken neck in the weeds on the side of the highway four miles outside of Vegas. Clearly he'd died elsewhere and someone had moved him, but nobody could figure out why or who.

Vegas was a mob town, a racially charged town. Money ruled. Sex, alcohol and power played heavily, too. With so many poisons running through its green veins, it's hard to imagine its white police force pursuing the ugly truth about the death of a young black man, even one of Gray's visibility and renown. The autopsy describes Gray's injury as a "fracture of the 5th and 6th cervical vertebrae with resultant injury to the spiral cord" and "contusion of the brain due to blow on head," or at least the novelized version does. To the question of how the injury occurred, the death certificate states: "Fall on cement floor." Wardell was buried in Detroit, Michigan where he grew up. The Las Vegas police closed the case.

People speculated: murder, racism, a love triangle, drugs. Maybe the white powers that be were trying to stop a black business of that size from succeeding. The Moulin Rouge did close within a year of opening. Either way, "Fall on cement floor" seemed too easy an explanation for the loss of someone this talented.

In *West Coast Jazz,* Ted Gioia provides a verifiable account of Gray's death. Like many jazz players at the time, Gray had started using heroin. Overdoses killed many of them, including pianist Sonny Clark and saxophonist Ernie Henry. Some people suspected Gray owed drug dealers money. Others speculated that he'd been messing around with another person's wife or girlfriend and got snuffed out. According to a dancer friend who was partying with Wardell on the night of the final shows, Gray shot heroin and fell off his bed, breaking his neck. Instead of trying to revive him or find medical help, he panicked. As bassist Red Callender put it: "If the guys he was with had any brains they would have taken him to a hospital, they could have saved him. Instead, he died and they dumped him in the desert. . . .Had he lived he would have been one of the truly amazing players of our time. He was anyhow."

Gray died on May 25, 1955. I was born on May 25, 1975. I was raised in Phoenix, Arizona, and I know the desert Gray died in well. Since I discovered his music, I've tried to take a moment to think of him on my birthday, not the waste of his life, but the success of it. He packed a lot in, so I privately pause to acknowledge that he walked the earth long enough to leave a tail of moving music as long as Haley's Comet, a tail which still streaks our mortal skies, even as he passed around the curve of this earth, out into the darkness.

At the Piano:
Remembering Lorraine Geller and Portland's Jazz History

In 1954, twenty-six year old jazz pianist Lorraine Geller recorded what would be her sole album as a leader: *Lorraine Geller at the Piano*. She worked hard and played widely with big names like Miles Davis and Philly Joe Jones. Her touch was firm and elegant, her solos full of complex ideas and shifting moods, and she could cook on the fast songs. Along with pianists Jutta Hipp, Mary Lou Williams and Mary McPartland, she was one of the few female instrumentalists playing in this male-dominated, mid-century genre. A week after playing the first Monterey Jazz Festival in 1958, she died from pulmonary edema. She was thirty years old. Her album *At the Piano* has long since fallen out of print in the US, but if you love piano trios, you need this album. Right now it's only available as a Japanese import, but Universal Music Group, which owns Dot Records' masters, needs to rerelease it so people other than collectors can afford to buy it.

Lorraine Winifred Walsh packed a lot of music into her short life. Born in Portland, Oregon in 1928, she grew up sketching and reading poetry and played classical piano. Her family lived somewhere on Ankeny Street in southeast Portland, in a neighborhood filled with houses now too expensive for many musicians to afford. Back in the 1920s, though, Portland wasn't a gentrifying city. It was a two-horse town known for its flooded river banks and unreliable bridges. People called it Stumptown and Mudtown, depending on what they tripped over. But the completion of Bonneville Dam in 1937 made the mighty Columbia River more navigable. The growth of logging, fishing and burgeoning shipyards in the 1940s drew people to Portland's growing economy, particularly African Americans, and as jazz started gaining popularity throughout America, a thriving jazz scene arose in a racially segregated part of inner north Portland that became known as Jumptown.

Portland was once one of the most segregated cities outside of the South. Forced out and prohibited from buying property in many areas because of redlining and other outlawed practices, people of color raised families and ran their own businesses in Portland's lower Albina neighborhood and what became The Rose Quarter. Many of the bars and clubs along Williams, Mississippi and Vancouver avenues hosted jazz. In venues like the Uptown Ballroom, The Dude Ranch, McClendon's Rhythm Room and The Chicken Coop, bands played late into the night, giving the neighborhood a bustling, big city energy that attracted well-known touring musicians like Louis

Armstrong, Count Basie, Oscar Peterson and Wardell Gray. As Robert Dietsche writes in his book *Jumptown: The Golden Years of Portland Jazz 1942-1957*: "Action central was Williams Avenue, an entertainment strip lined with hot spots where you could find jazz twenty-four hours a day. ...You could stand in the middle of the Avenue (where the Blazers play basketball today) and look up Williams past the chili parlors, past the barbecue joints, the beauty salons, all the way to Broadway, and see hundreds of people dressed up as if they were going to a fashion show. It could be four in the morning. It didn't matter; this was one of those 'streets that never slept.'"

In 1940, trumpeter Erskine Hawkins' dance band played downtown at McElroy's Spanish Ballroom. Located on Southwest 5th Avenue between Madison and Main, many stars played there during its heyday, from Duke Ellington to John Coltrane to Cab Calloway, earning it the reputation as Portland's Cotton Club. The difference was, McElroy's was in the white part of town. It was west of the Willamette River. Black Portland gathered to the east. Many downtown businesses refused people of color, just like the city's banks refused people of color loans, but Cole McElroy welcomed everyone as customers by hosting "mixed dance" at his ballroom. In Jumptown, jazz and black community thrived. At McElroy's, the races mingled on the dance floor, and Portland's white audiences could discover new songs and new jazz musicians in what they probably considered a "safe"—meaning white—environment.

After Erskine Hawkins' show, his record "After Hours" sold well in town, and the song played regularly on the jukebox at a joint called Slaughters. Lorraine Walsh was young and white, but she heard Erskine's song and often went to hear people play at clubs like Jackie's Cafe and Acme, especially a Be Bop and boogie-woogie pianist named Leo "Dark Eyes" Amadee. Lorraine's band director at Washington High School had introduced her to jazz, and she'd started listening to cutting edge pianists like Bud Powell, Thelonious Monk and Art Tatum, and soon she refocused her classical piano education on jazz. Her mother was very supportive. "After Hours" seems to have made a strong enough impression on the young pianist to solidify her dedication to jazz. Her friend Jeannie Hackett remembers going to record stores with Lorraine, hunting for Gene Krupa and Nat King Cole albums. "I don't know why," Hackett says in *Jumptown*, "but Lorraine always liked Krupa's pianist, Teddy Napoleon." In 1942, Lorraine played in a boogie-woogie quartet at a Franklin High School assembly. Sixteen years later, she became what Dietsche calls "The most highly acclaimed pianist in Portland jazz history". Sad, then, that so few people, including Portlanders, have heard of her.

You have to wonder what talented Portland pianists of color never had the opportunity or money to visit a recording studio. As Ralph Ellison writes in "The Charlie

Christian Story" in 1958, many of jazz's "heroes remain local figures known only to small-town dance halls, and whose reputations are limited to the radius of a few hundred miles." The musicians we know, he argues, are not simply the ones with the most talent. They're the ones who got lucky, got noticed, got into a studio. "Some of the most brilliant of jazzmen made no records," says Ellison, "their names appeared in print only in announcement of some local dance or remote 'battles of music' against equally uncelebrated bands. Being devoted to an art which traditionally thrives on improvisation, these unrecorded artists very often have their most original ideas enter the public domain almost as rapidly as they are conceived, to be quickly absorbed into the thought and technique of their fellows. Thus, the riffs which swung the dancers and the band on some transcendent evening, and which inspired others to competitive flights of invention, become all too swiftly a part of the general style, leaving the originator as anonymous as the creators of the architecture called Gothic." So which Portlanders of color would have joined Geller in the upper ranks of Portland's best if they'd had the same access as white players and weren't systematically oppressed? In mid-century jazz, those who we know as the best aren't always measured by talent or innovation, but by having the privilege of leaving a document. This isn't to undermine Geller's standing or suggest she's undeserving of recognition. She is brilliant. Context is complicated.

She's one of my favorite pianists. But surely there were others in Jumptown who played extremely well.

•

Lorraine's career developed quickly. From 1949 to 1952, she played with an all-female big band named the Sweethearts of Rhythm. Led by vocalist Anna Mae Winburn, its earlier incarnation was the first racially integrated all female-group in America, had toured widely and garnered a big following. Although this period of Lorraine's musical life is hazy, in 1949, she found herself in Los Angeles jamming with an alto saxophonist named Herb Geller.

Herb was born in LA and played saxophone at Dorsey High School with fellow saxophonists Eric Dolphy and Vi Redd, who both went on to fame. After seeing Charlie Parker and Dizzy Gillespie perform in LA in 1945, Herb went so wild for bop that he moved to New York City to put himself in the center of this new music. Herb was always looking for work, so he joined as many late-night jam sessions as he could. These were standard practice at the time, with jazz musicians cramming into apartments or in clubs until dawn, blowing and vamping and even competing, which made it a great way to make friends and forge professional relationships, and to write songs. While touring, he met Lorraine at one LA jam session in 1949. They hit it off and kept playing together, and romance blossomed. Herb was playing with Billy May's and Claude Thornhill's orchestras in New York, so he and Lorraine moved there in the fall of 1952 and got married. That year, she played with trumpeter Norma Carson's all-female group, which did a brief residency at The Welcome Bar in Atlantic City. When May's band relocated to Los Angeles in 1953, the Gellers did too, and they built themselves into in-demand players.

As the *JazzTimes* put it: "For the next half-decade, the Gellers were integral participants in the heyday of so-called West Coast jazz." They did studio work to make money. They played shows at night and recorded albums during the day, joining big names like Clifford Brown, Red Mitchell and Dinah Washington. And they formed their own quartet, called The Gellers, which released three albums in 1954 and '55. In 1955, they moved into a nice house in the Hollywood Hills.

During her Los Angeles years, Lorraine alone played with a who's-who of West Coast jazz, including Zoot Sims, Stan Getz, Red Mitchell, and even Charlie Parker and Dizzy Gillespie. But the jazz life was inconsistent. Lorraine took gigs in strip clubs to make money. Lots of people did. It was a booming supplemental market. As pianist Dick Whittington told Ted Gioia in *West Coast Jazz*, during some of the 1950s, "The bottom dropped out so far as jazz work was concerned...there were probably ten strip joints in LA, and they would hire a three-piece band. They'd have saxophone, piano, and drums. No bass—they didn't feel they needed that. They just wanted a melody and the rhythm, especially that drum beat. Everyone worked strip gigs. Hampton Hawes, Carl Perkins, Walter Norris, Herb and Lorraine Geller."

One of the most important developments in her career was the rise of a club in Hermosa Beach called The Lighthouse. In 1949, the bar's owner let bassist Howard Rumsey host a regular Saturday night jam session there; when it became popular, Rumsey became club manager, and he built the place into one of the centers of West Coast jazz from the 1950s to the '70s. Touring bands played there. Record labels recorded live albums there. The club even birthed its own group called—blandly—the Lighthouse All-Stars. Early iterations featured saxophonists Gerry Mulligan and Sonny Criss, with pianists Sonny Clark and Hampton Hawes. One version included Lorraine.

When the famous bop drummer Max Roach came from New York to temporarily replace the Lighthouse's house drummer in 1953, he brought Miles Davis and Charles Mingus with him. On Roach's first night playing the venue on September 13, both Davis and Chet Baker played trumpet together. Davis famously disliked Baker (you can see this in Ethan Hawke's movie about him, *Born to Be Blue*), and this was the only time the two played music together. Lorraine provided the piano. A fan recorded the show. It took thirty-two years for the tapes to surface officially, and the recording, titled *At Last!*, captures a hard-hitting Geller playing over an overly hard-hitting Max Roach on drums.

In 1957, Lorraine recorded with California bassist Red Mitchell on what was her most commercially successful date. But her trio is her greatest showcase. Even though Lorraine's soloing on Red's date is great, the set sounds boring and staid, the songs overly familiar. Unfortunately, this marks the end of Lorraine's ascent.

That year, she was diagnosed with asthma. When she gave birth to her daughter Lisa, Lisa had developmental issues, and the birth strained Lorraine's health. While Lisa stayed in the hospital for six months under supervision, Lorraine recuperated. Insurance wouldn't cover Lisa's treatment. With medical bills mounting, the Gellers cashed in their life insurance policy, and Lorraine started playing with singer Kay Starr. "I have to do it," she told Herb, "we need the money." When Herb got invited to tour with Benny Goodman, he jumped at the chance. He rehearsed in New York, embarked on the tour. The soon-to-be-famous Monterey Jazz Festival debuted with a stellar line-up, and Lorraine played it. Then in October, 1958, Lorraine came down with a pulmonary infection. Her lungs filled with fluid. She had an asthma attack, and she died. Herb was on the road with Goodman when his mother called. "I could hear in her voice that something was wrong," he recalled. "She said, 'Herb, Lorraine died.'" Her death disoriented him. "After the funeral in L.A., I was devastated and had no idea what to do. Lorraine had been my entire life. But I had to go back to work to make ends meet. I called Benny Goodman's office and said I'd like to come back with the band. Benny called me and was as nice as can be. He said, 'Herb, you left a big hole in the band. Please come back.'"

Herb's sister watched Lisa so he could finish the tour. Depressed and confused, he bounced gig to gig for a few years, cobbling together an income in a patchwork of towns, but he was lost. "At one point I was playing at this [strip] club in West Hollywood called the Pink Pussycat," he remembered. "One night, a girl I knew said to me that a dear friend wanted to see me. I was in the middle of playing *Night Train*. Suddenly I felt a hand on my shoulder. I looked up. It was Stan Getz." Getz played "Night Train" as part of his repertoire. He'd had his own ups and downs. "At intermission Stan said, 'Why don't you go to Europe. You shouldn't be playing strip clubs. I know a guy at the Montmartre Club in Copenhagen who will give you a gig there.'" So Herb sold his and Lorraine's house and bought a ticket to Copenhagen. After some detours, he eventually settled in Germany and played jazz in Europe for the rest of his life.

Where Herb left Lisa and America behind (his sister eventually adopted her), Lorraine left behind a daughter, a devastated husband, and one of the most under-recognized gems of piano jazz. *At the Piano* is a high-water mark of the trio format, and one of my personal favorites. If Portland has one jazz album to brag about, it's this.

Recorded in LA in 1954, *At the Piano* came out in 1959, a year after Lorraine died. Jazz trios are a dime a dozen, and piano trio albums can sound so much alike that they seem interchangeable. The worst have too many standards. Too little fire. Not enough swing. They can sound stiff, safe, almost classical in their polish. Lorraine's, though, brims with life.

At the Piano includes surprising cover songs and four of her original compositions, memorable and moving with names like "Clash By Night" and "Madame X;" these songs double as glimpses of what her future held. Bassist Leroy Vinnegar played on it. Self-taught, he was one of the West Coast's most active and unique bass-players, known for a signature walking bass line. Interestingly, Vinnegar moved to Portland in 1986 and spent the rest of his life here. The Oregon State Legislature honored him by naming May 1st Leroy Vinnegar Day. In 2002, pianist and educator Darrell Grant built on by establishing the Leroy Vinnegar Jazz Institute at Portland State University. Vinnegar and Geller lock in tight on the album. Since the album's only thirty-two minutes long, its fire leaves you wanting more, which of course can be said of Lorraine's whole musical life.

•

If Lorraine's professional experience was like Jutta Hipp's and Mary Lou Williams', and it likely was, then many people took Lorraine less seriously than her male counterparts. Men likely focused on her looks. They expected less of her, talked down to her, and marveled when she could play what men considered standard, because she was a woman. Case in point: The record label turned the piano on her album cover into a high heel. In *Jumptown*, one of her band mates, Earl Whitney, describes a time he declined a gig because of sexism.

> We'd got this call for an audition at the Tropics Club so we went out there and played. When it was over, the owner called me over to the bar and said, 'You kids sound nice, but the girl doesn't look good on stage. She's gotta go.' He never said anything about the way she played.

> I didn't take the job of course, and I never told Lorraine about it. She was just one of the guys to us. In fact, we all called her 'man.' It must have gotten under her skin though, 'cause one day she called me over and said, 'Look, Earl, I'm no man, I'm a woman.' From then on we called her 'Jazz.' Pretty soon everybody in town was calling her that.

Twenty-first century Portland is a bustling gentrifying

metropolis filled with musicians and writers and the creative class. No longer Mudtown, it's known for world class food and the arts. Even though the state is becoming more ethnically diverse, central Portland is still racially divided and predominantly white. Its progressive populace talks and votes like we value diversity and equality, and many businesses and leaders here are showing the world how gender equality looks. Yet Portland has no memorial for Lorraine Geller. There's no sign or plaque commemorating her artistic accomplishments, no evidence of her existence at all. When I called one of our popular local jazz clubs to ask about her, the owner didn't recognize her name. Neither did the manager at the small record shop I asked. It isn't surprising. She had one solo record, and this is jazz we're talking about. It's obscure. But Portland has a statue for Beverly Clearly, author of the Ramona books, as they should. Cleary's Ramona character shaped many young readers' lives, and she continues to. Maybe Geller didn't live long enough to build the sort of catalog that demands attention. Maybe jazz trios can never have the same emotional effect that stories do. But Portland's greatest jazz pianist deserves at least a small plaque honoring her. The same goes for Jumptown.

"By the early 1960s," Jeffrey Showell writes in The Oregonian, "much of the [Jumptown] area had been razed to build Memorial Coliseum and Lloyd Center. Interstate 5, known as the Minnesota Freeway because it was built over the route of North Minnesota Avenue, cut through the heart of the Albina neighborhood and resulted in the destruction of scores of residential blocks." The old clubs were torn down, light rail tracks laid, Emanual Hospital built, and part of the area dubbed The Rose Quarter. The Blazers play there now. People catch commuter trains. Otherwise, between game days, it's a vacant quarter. The lack of night life and businesses obscures every bit of its lively, musical, African-American roots. Only one of the old jazz venues survives. Called The Dude Ranch, this two-story wedge of old brick stands between two busy one-way streets. It's a mixed use space now, with offices, a brewery and a bakery, and few passing drivers probably know what it was, or that Thelonious Monk and Coleman Hawkins played there together, or that Nat King Cole and Art Tatum played there, or that visitors danced and kissed and celebrated life. I only learned about it this year and I'm a huge jazz fan. I've passed it for sixteen years.

The people of color who lived in this neighborhood who raised their families and made their livings here, lost it to the real estate investors who bought Williams Avenue only to tear it down, while the city boosters carved up Jumptown with what was dubbed "urban renewal" and left it divided and conquered, its insides exposed. So where is their memorial? How is their existence and their legacy being honored? There are books about the Albina area's history. There are organizations and neighborhood groups. But this community's history deserves larger public recognition. Instead, they have holes to stare into.

A block of beautiful buildings once stood on Williams Avenue and Russell Street. Called the Hill Block, it was filled with black businesses and bustling traffic. There's a crisp 1962 photograph of it, showing cars and pedestrians and life. Emanual Hospital bought the lot for a planned expansion but ran out of money after clearing it for construction. The lot has sat vacant for over two decades. In place of people and businesses, wood chips and weeds now fill the lot.

In the early 2000s, a scheme was floated to rebrand The Rose Quarter as the "Jumptown" entertainment district. The new Jumptown would mix retail, hotel, restaurant and residential, but that plan was what city Commissioner Randy Leonard called "the Walmart of entertainment." The firm involved had a contentious history with the African-American community, with claims of racist dress codes on a past redevelopment project, and over all, it was an insult to name a new pre-fab development 'Jumptown' after the namesake was destroyed for the benefit of the white majority. No surprise, though, for this is jazz. You can't talk about jazz without talking about race relations and tragedy, glory and creativity, money and beauty, economic disparities between musicians and businesses, celebration, struggle and death.

As Geoff Dyer says in his jazz book, *But Beautiful*:

"Anyone who becomes interested in jazz is struck very early on by the high casualty rate of its practitioners." It's clichéd to ask what Lorraine Geller could have done if she'd lived longer—all the songs she could have written, the albums she would have released. People ask the same about clean-living trumpeter Clifford Brown, who died in a 1956 car accident at age twenty-five. They ask the same about trumpeter Booker Little, who died from uremia at age twenty-three. Same with vibraphonist Eddie Costa, killed in a crash in 1962. Same with pianist Vince Guaraldi, who had a heart attack in his hotel room between performances, and with Herb Geller's high school friend Eric Dolphy, who died suddenly in 1964 of a diabetic coma, after hospital staff assumed he was a drug addict rather than a diabetic. It's a familiar question, but it's a legitimate one. Imagine their lives and what could have been. Herb lived until age eighty-five. What music would Lorraine have made had she lived? Like the song "All the Things You Are," Lorraine's recorded work is many things, most of it great, but her best performances on *At the Piano*, like Jumptown's existence, were so brief that when the world turned its head for just a moment, we missed them. The time has come to turn our head back.

Five Days of Jazz
in New York City

My plane from Oregon landed at LaGuardia at 5:15 p.m., less than two hours before tenor saxophonist Jimmy Heath's concert started in Harlem's Marcus Garvey Park. Heath was eighty-six. He'd written jazz standards such as "C.T.A." and "For Minors Only," and he'd played with everyone from Miles Davis to Kenny Dorham. Tonight he was leading a big band as part of New York City's annual Charlie Parker Jazz Festival. The free concert's organizer advised people to arrive early. An hour before show time wasn't unreasonable. The City Parks Foundation expected over three thousand attendants, and I intended to be one of them.

I hadn't come to New York to hear jazz. I'd come on business. As a jazz fan, though, when one of my favorite musicians plays, I make time. When else would I get the chance? Even as the ranks of jazz's living legends thinned, giants still played New York City in such numbers that you couldn't make all their gigs. Over the next five days, there were a total of six jazz concerts I wanted to see. Jimmy Heath's younger, seventy-eight year old drummer brother

'Tootie' was playing The Village Vanguard. Eighty-five year old saxophonist Lee Konitz was playing a free quartet show in Tompkins Square Park. Miles Davis drummer Jimmy Cobb's trio was also playing The Vanguard. Saxophone star Kenny Garrett was playing for free in Harlem, and pianist Junior Mance was at a Midtown club called Kitano. These guys were brilliant. When Coltrane got sober and recorded his first album as a leader, the 1957 masterpiece *Coltrane*, Tootie backed him on drums. That cymbal crash that leads into Miles Davis' famous song "So What"? One of jazz's most famous? Cobb hit that. He'd toured with Davis' classic quintet when it included Cannonball Adderley, Paul Chambers, Wynton Kelly and Coltrane, and he'd drummed behind Coltrane and guitarist Kenny Burrell on the only album they recorded together. This is how I rationalized having to see them all perform. Cobb and Mance might still play regularly around New York, but as a West Coast resident, that didn't do me much good. Also, Cobb and Mance were eighty-four. Musicians never know how much longer their bodies will allow them to play.

Pianist Ahmad Jamal was planning to retire from performing. Pianist Cedar Walton passed away four days earlier, at age seventy-nine. I saw Walton perform back home in Portland, Oregon in May, 2012. In fact, his trio just played The Village Vanguard last month. As if to honor what were likely his final shows, the Vanguard kept the info up on their website: "Cedar Walton-p," it said,

"David Williams-b, George Fludas-d, July 09 - July 14." Knowing any day could be our last, when I travel, I do as my mom does: too much. "Cram it all in," she likes to say, "but slow down enough to enjoy it." I also heed actress Mae West: "Too much of a good thing is wonderful!" So I penciled six shows into my schedule and raced to get to the first one.

LaGuardia sprawls across northern Queens, four miles from Manhattan. Unlike JFK Airport, no subways serve LaGuardia directly. I took the public bus.

The M60 bus ran straight through Queens to Harlem's 125th Street, one block north of the park. An airport clerk said the ride could take thirty to forty-five minutes in rush-hour traffic. Hoping for the best, I crammed onto the long accordion bus alongside countless commuters. Facing front to back, multiple hands gripping the same poles for stability, our bodies bumped each other with seemingly every sharp turn and tap of the brakes, as the bus wobbled toward Manhattan.

The city's skyline shifted in and out of view, filling my body with worry and excitement with each glimpse. Would I make the concert? Would traffic or some horrendous car accident prevent my arrival? Standing among commuters, I plotted how I would get from one concert to the next, how much time I had between the end of one performance and the start of the next, and which streets to walk between venues and which subways to take. Mance and Garrett played on the same days; so did Cobb and Konitz. I had what you could call an abundance of greatness. It was a nice problem to have.

The bus squeaked to a halt. So many people filled the interior that few could board at the first stop. Two people squeezed in through a rear door and caused a ruckus with an older man in a suit. He stood in the rear vestibule and wouldn't move for a man in a blue polo shirt and jeans. "Please," the second man said, pushing his way on. "It's okay. I got this." He did. The man in the suit had room to give but seemed resistant on philosophical grounds: he'd paid; this man should have to, too. They faced each other in the doorway, squaring off as the sliding door clicked and clicked, unable to close.

"Let that door close, now," the bus driver said. "Work it out." A young passenger further back raised a fist as affirmation.

With people watching, the two warring men finally shifted for the door and stood side by side for the next few stops, avoiding each other's eyes.

Plain brick apartment buildings and car repair shops passed outside as we sped down Astoria Boulevard. Standing in the pivoting joint that connected the double bus's sections, I thought about the other jazz greats I'd seen play. My first real jazz concert was also in New York: Sonny Rollins, end of summer 2006, outside Lincoln Center. I'd just gotten into Hard bop jazz a few years earlier, and there I was, sitting feet from one of its most inventive practitioners, in the city that helped birth this music. It was an auspicious start to my life as a jazz fan.

After Rollins, I attended any show I could. I saw trombonist Curtis Fuller play at Minton's in Harlem. Fuller had played on Coltrane's *Blue Train*. In concert, he wore a ballcap that said "Old School." I saw drummer Jimmy Cobb play with Wes Montgomery's organist Melvin Rhyne at Small's in the West Village; Cobb's daughter sat on the bar stool beside me, studying flash cards for an upcoming test. When I asked Cobb if I could film some of the show on my phone, he responded in a raspy suspicious voice: "For what?" I said, as a memento of one my happiest musical experiences. He studied me a moment, unconvinced. I promised I wouldn't post it online; I just wanted to be able to watch it again. With one hand on a drum stick and one squinting eye on me, he raised a thumbs up and said, "Cool, man. You got it." Another time I saw reclusive pianist Freddie Redd perform his classic soundtrack to the film *The Connection* with soulful alto Lou Donaldson and drummer Louis Hayes; Redd hadn't played the full set in decades. These ranked as some of the highlights of my musical life. I wanted more. Morbid as it seemed, the players' age imparted a sense of urgency, a sentiment captured in Charlie Parker's 1945 song title "Now's the Time." That or I might have become one of those obsessive jazz collector types, the kind who, like birders, were compelled to check items they'd "seen" off of lists. That was okay, too.

"Thirty-first Street," the bus driver said.

After the bus crossed the East River, a Bronx woman and I started talking. I told her about the show and she asked if I'd eaten dinner. I hadn't. "What do you like?" she said. Korean, Mexican, Puerto Rican, Japanese, soul, I answered. She suggested a soul food place called Manna's and gave me directions. "Take it to go," she said, "eat it at the park. Enjoy that music."

I carried Manna's take-out through the park and found a bench ten rows from the front. Barely half the seats were filled by 6:25. Black and white, young and old, scholarly looking people in thick glasses and button-ups sat beside men in Army veteran ball-caps and t-shirts. Many attendees wore bright clothes decorated with ornate beadwork; others wore silky collared shirts or dresses suited to an expensive dinner at the Waldorf Astoria.

The warm summer air cooled as the sun set, and the rest of the seats filled. The park's seating area held about 2500 people; the area reached capacity by 6:45. By the time Jimmy Heath and his band took the stage, some four thousand listeners spread throughout the park, spilling out from the amphitheater, into the adjacent lawns and walkways, often out of view of the stage but within earshot. I'd barely made it.

Heath led a seventeen-piece band. The audience erupted in applause as Heath stepped to the edge of the stage to address them. "I would like to say that we'd like to dedicate this program this evening," he said, his voice buoyant and scratchy, "to one of my dear friends, Mr. Cedar Walton, who just passed."

Countless cell phone and long lens cameras went up to capture this historic event. Wearing a green vest over a black shirt and slacks, he divided the set into two sections. The first consisted of an original piece he composed for the event, a multi-part Charlie Parker-themed song that the Parks Foundation commissioned, called "Bird is the Word." For the second half, the band played Parker songs that they adapted to the big band format.

"This is one that Charlie Parker wrote *waaaay* back," Heath said deep into the set. "I heard it when I was a kid. It was Charlie Parker and Tiny Grimes, the guitarist, and it's called 'Red Cross.'" They followed that with "Parker's Mood" and his classic, "Yardbird Suite."

Couples in white suits and nice dresses danced by the stage. A little girl jumped around and kicked her legs, facing the audience so everyone could see. An elderly man in a black cap emblazoned with "Harlem" yelled "Pluck it like Mingus!" I wedged my luggage under the seat so I could tap my feet without rubbing the canvas.

When Heath wasn't soloing, he conducted the band, waving his hands and pointing to instrumentalists to solo, raise the volume, fade in and out. One difference between his leadership and that of a classical music conductor: he danced while doing it. Heath clapped. He slid his shoes across the stage's smooth surface, and he shimmied with his arms held out, as if the music had set him aloft. Even from ten rows back, you could see the ever-present smile on his face. He lived for this music, *his* music, and that of Parker and Walton, and those who Heath called "all the greats."

Forget the concert play-by-play. Forget which songs the band performed in what order, how the interpretations sounded and which of the four trombonist players soloed on which part. I scribbled this information down in a notebook. I wanted to remember the details, from the set list to Heath's comments to the ways audience members responded. I'm a sentimental documentarian. I fill pages with observations. But by the band's second song, these details no longer mattered. Only the general mood mattered, and the mood was jubilant, communal and summery. People attend concerts for many reasons. One is the feeling the collective experience of live music produces. Heath's show struck me like an improvised sax solo: you might not remember the exact sequence of notes or the melody the musician played, but you remember the overall effect the solo had on you, how the sound made you *feel*, and that was enough.

Heath's posture told me all I needed to know: he shook his butt with the sway of Carmen Miranda because he radiated this music, and he transmitted that enthusiasm to listeners. Thousands of strangers bobbed their heads to the rhythm and clapped our hands together. We howled "Play that thing, play it!" and traded excited glances during heated trumpet solos. A solitary man with a cane sat next to me, smacking his thin, wrinkled thigh in sync with the drums, and I stood up to dance in the aisle during one song. This is why I go to hear live music. This is why I booked five other shows. The concert signaled a strong start to a week of New York jazz. People danced and clapped and yelled "Woo, hoo!" This is what music is meant to do.

Writing with Miles Davis

If Miles Davis's mid-century trumpet solos can be described by a single phrase, it might be "doing more with less." Despite his renown, Davis wasn't a flashy or highly technical player during the late 1950s and early '60s. He was melodic and economical, and his approach can teach prose writers a lot about the power of concision, suggestion and space.

It's difficult to characterize music in simple, sweeping terms. Davis explored numerous styles in a catalog that spanned decades; change defined him as much as his Harmon mute. But in the 1950s he started moving away from the early Be Bop of his mentor and band mate Charlie Parker to explore a leaner sound. Rather than squeezing as many notes and changes into solos as possible, Davis dispensed with clutter and ornamentation and pared his mode of expression down to one defined as much by the notes and phrases he played as by the silences left between them. As the critic Stanley Crouch observed: "Part of his genius as a musician was that he edited what he heard Charlie Parker play."

Where David Foster Wallace showed writers like me the

possibilities of labyrinthine stories and digressions, Davis showed me how to be affecting without being opaque, lyrical without being verbose. Editing imbued each of Davis's notes with more weight. It also let his melodic lines breathe, an effect that highlighted the depth and strength of his lyricism. No matter the tempo, Davis's precise, deft touch produced solos whose moods ranged from buoyant to brooding, mournful to sweet.

Many writers fall prey to the quintessential American notion that bigger is better. They overload their sentences, adding more adjectives, more descriptions, more component phrases, tangents and appositives to form sprawling, syntactical centipedes (like this one) whose many segments and exhausting procession repeat themselves and say the same thing in different ways, with different words, and exhibit an entire ideology: that prose's sensory and poetic impacts exist in direct proportion to the concentration of words. I know: I succumbed.

For many years I was impressed by flamboyant displays like the 255-word sentence in the journalist Marshall Frady's essay "South Domesticated," a monument to excess held together with only three dashes.

Calvin Trillin's sinuous, compound sentences also enchanted me. The problem was that when I aped Trillin's style, I imitated only his long sentences, not the short ones he interspersed. This disparity gave my early essays a manic quality that frazzled the nerves and tired quickly.

Something about youth draws many of us to maximalism: Hunter S. Thompson, Jack Kerouac, Terry Southern, Tom Wolfe. Maybe the style—the sentences' wildness, decadence and audacity—mirrors youth itself. The opening line of Southern's novel "Candy" seemed to confirm to me that iconic stylists are the ones who pen mouthfuls: "'I've read *many* books,' said Professor Mephesto, with an odd finality, wearily flattening his hands on the podium, addressing the seventy-six sophomores who sat in easy reverence, immortalizing his every phrase with their pads and pens, and now, as always, giving him the confidence to slowly, artfully dramatize his words, to pause, shrug, frown, gaze abstractly at the ceiling, allow a wan wistful smile to play at his lips, and repeat quietly, '*many* books.'"

Yet the more I listened to Davis's music, the more his approach started to influence my writing style. His solos in "Diane" and "It Could Happen to You" show how measured, uncluttered phrasing increases rather than decreases the impact. Unlike so much fat-cat prose, Davis's solos didn't divert from their emotional center by wowing the audience with speed and facility. With less distraction, the force of his music landed more squarely on me.

I started to experiment with economy as a form, hanging fewer phrases and images on the white walls of my essays. I also began to seek out writers who utilized this sparse style. Take Abigail Thomas. In a career spanning six books, Thomas has distinguished herself, in part, by her brevity. She begins her memoir "A Three Dog Life" with succinct, meticulous bursts: "This is the one thing that stays the same: my husband got hurt. Everything else changes. A grandson needs me and then he doesn't. My children are close then one drifts away. I smoke and don't smoke; I knit ponchos, then hats, shawls, hats again, stop knitting, start up again. The clock ticks, the seasons shift, the night sky rearranges itself, but my husband remains constant, his injuries are permanent."

Like Davis's trumpet, Thomas's short sentences create mood. Structurally, she spins an ingenious centrifuge to take readers through the whirlwind of her confusion and despair. Beginning with blunt declarations, she builds momentum with a list and then uses commas to amplify the pace and tension, creating turbulent whitecaps on the flat, sullen surface of her introductory statement.

Davis's saxophonist Cannonball Adderley once described him as "the type of soloist who implies a lot of things." What is left unsaid colors much of Tony Earley's book "Somehow Form a Family." To describe his poor family's character Earley chooses basic, unadorned details: "Our clothes were clean. My parents worked. We went to church. Easter mornings, Mama stood us in front of the yellowbell bush and took our picture." I don't know what a yellowbell bush is, but I know that these people are upstanding, proud, independent, tight-knit, without the writer's spelling it out.

Some of Raymond Carver's best writing also operates in the realm of suggestion. Describing his father's 1934 departure from Arkansas in search of work, Carver wrote: "I don't know whether he was pursuing a dream when he went out to Washington. I doubt it. I don't think he dreamed much." The impact of these short sentences stems less from mood or tension as bluntness. His brevity registers as acceptance, a pragmatic, maybe even disappointing, shrug at life's deprivations: *It's unfortunate, but that's how Dad was.* At least, that's how I interpret the passage. It's also how suggestion works. Brevity often invites speculation and facilitates a dynamic interaction between reader and writing.

Listening to Davis taught me these things. He also underscored the value of experimentation and reinvention, the fact that it was all right to change, to try new styles, even when evolution meant abandoning your old comfortable routines, or worse, forsaking peoples' favorites. Even though I don't particularly like the musical directions he took later in life, I admire his need to explore, to test the limits of his form and himself. "The way you change and help music," Davis said, "is by trying to invent new ways to play." Every day I sit down at the computer, I try to remember that.

Acknowledgments

The following essays appeared in these publications: "Jimmy Smith and the Allure of the Vault" and "Four Nights of Jazz in New York City" in *The Threepenny Review*; "Don't Worry 'Bout Me: The Brief Career and Self-Imposed Exile of Jutta Hipp, Jazz Pianist" in *Apology*; "When It Was New: Miles Davis' 'So What'" in *AGNI*; "What Is and What Could Be: Hank Mobley" in *Conjunctions*; "Eulogy for Lee" in *Paris Review* Daily; "This Is" in *Kenyon Review*; "Unapologetic Vision: Miles Davis and the Lesson of 'Sid's Ahead'" and "Among the Throngs: The Legacy of Lucky Thompson" in *Brick*; "The Lost Footage of Pianist Sonny Clark," "Jazz Fiction and Reality: The Bright Comet of Wardell Gray" and "At the Piano: Lorraine Geller" on the *Michigan Quarterly Review* Blog; "Writing with Miles Davis" in *The New York Times*. My eternal gratitude to the editors Wendy Lesser, Jesse Pearson, Nadia Szilvassy, Liz Johnston, Sergei Lobanov-Rostovsky, Whitney Dangerfield, Brad Morrow, Micaela Morrissette, Sadie Stein, Sven Birkerts, Bill Pierce and Rachell Farrell whose careful eyes and thoughtful edits improved these stories and first brought them to readers.

A huge and special thanks to Katja von Schuttenbach for sharing her time and some of her research on Jutta Hipp with me. Jutta is fortunate to have Katja as her advocate. Thanks to Tom Evered for sharing his experience at Blue Note, and to Dr. Wolfram Knauer and Doris Schröder at the Jazzinstitut Darmstadt for helping me utilize their robust German archives. Huge thanks to Ol' Eagle Eye McFadden for cleaning up my mess. You walk the sacred path of the burrito, the book and the LP like a true original. I see more movies in our future. A big, big thanks to the generous writers and musicians who read this manuscript before I first published it to offer an encouraging blurb.

And finally, my love to my parents, who showed me the way through music and put it in the blood. That's where it will remain, and you with it. Us singing Bob Wills' "Take Me Back to Tulsa" on our family roadtrips, us singing Bing Crosby while decorating our artificial Christmas tree in Arizona, us singing Petula Clark's "Downtown" and Buck Owens and Ella Fitzgerald, and Dad pointing to the radio on our morning drive to school and asking, "Who's that?" and me answering: "Satchmo!" That's what music and you mean to me.

Works Cited

Here is a selection of works I utilized during the writing of this book. My thanks to all the authors whose research, ideas and enthusiasm contributed to my own.

Books

Ansell, Derek, *Workout: The Music of Hank Mobley.*
Asher, Don and Hawes, Hampton, *Raise Up Off Me: A Portrait of Hampton Hawes.*
Balliett, Whitney, *American Musicians II: Seventy-One Portraits in Jazz.*
Balliett, Whitney, *Jelly Roll, Jabbo & Fats: 19 Portraits in Jazz.*
Balliett, Whitney, *The Sound of Surprise: 46 Pieces on Jazz.*
Bjorn, Lars and Gallert, Jim, *Before Motown: A History of Jazz in Detroit, 1920-60.*
Carr, Ian, *Miles Davis: The Definitive Biography.*
Cook, Richard, *Blue Note Records: The Biography.*
Crouch, Stanley, *Considering Genius: Writings on Jazz.*
Dahl, Linda, *Stormy Weather: The Music and Lives of a Century of Jazz Women.*
DeVito, Chris, *Coltrane on Coltrane: The John Coltrane Interviews.*
Dietsche, Robert, *Jumptown: The Golden Years of Portland Jazz, 1942-1957.*
Dyer, Geoff, *But Beautiful: A Book About Jazz.*
Ellison, Ralph, *Shadow and Act.*
Feather, Leonard, *The Encyclopedia Yearbook of Jazz.*

Gelber, Jack, *The Connection: A Play.*

Gioia, Ted, *West Coast Jazz: Modern Jazz in California 1945-1960.*

Gold, Robert S., *Jazz Talk: A Dictionary of the Colorful Language That Has Emerged from America's Own Music.*

Gottlieb, Robert, *Reading Jazz: A Gathering of Autobiography, Reportage, and Criticism from 1919 to Now.*

Green, Sharony Andrews, *Grant Green: Rediscovering the Forgotten Genius of Jazz Guitar.*

Hentoff, Nat and Shapiro, Nat, *Hear Me Talkin' To Ya: The Story of Jazz As Told By the Men Who Made It.*

Kahn, Ashley, *Kind of Blue: The Making of the Miles Davis Masterpiece.*

Kunzler, Martin, *Jazz Lexikon.*

Mathieson, Kenny, *Cookin': Hard Bop and Soul Jazz 1954-65.*

Minor, William, *Jazz Journeys to Japan: The Heart Within.*

Moody, Bill, *Death of a Tenor Man.*

Morrison, Toni, *Jazz.*

Mosley, Walter, *Devil in a Blue Dress.*

Ondaatje, Michael, *Coming Through Slaughter.*

Ratliff, Ben, *Coltrane: The Story of a Sound.*

Roos, Roy E., *The History of Albina.*

Rosenthal, David H., *Hard Bop: Jazz & Black Music 1955-1965.*

Spencer, Frederick J., *Jazz and Death: Medical Profiles of Jazz Greats.*

Stephenson, Sam, *The Jazz Loft Project: Photographs and Tapes of W. Eugene Smith from 821 Sixth Avenue, 1957-1965.*

Taylor, Arthur, *Notes and Tones: Musician-to-Musician Interviews.*

Thomas, Abigail, *A Three Dog Life.*

Yanow, Scott, *Jazz on Film: The Complete Story of the Musicians and Music Onscreen.*

Articles, Essays, Recordings and Websites

Accardi, James and Varden, Stuart A. "Wardell Gray: The Many Faces of the Thin Man." http://www.wardellgray.org/

Balliett, Whitney. "Jazz Ten Levels." *The New Yorker*, August 16, 1982.

Christian Meier-Oehlke: Die Jazzmusikerin Jutta Hipp

Clarke, Shirley, *The Connection*, 1961.

Brecker, Daniel. Interview with Lucky Thompson, "Daniel Brecker's Jazz Family," KCMU-FM 1995.

Cohen, Noal and Byars, Chris. "Lucky Thompson In Paris: The 1961 Candid Records Session. *Current Research in Jazz 2*, 2010.

Cohen, Noal, liner notes for *Lucky Thompson – New York City, 1964-1965* CD, 2008.

Contreras, Felix. "Royalties Elusive For Many Jazz Greats." *NPR*, April 20, 2005.

Curtis' Jazz Cafe. "Unsung Women of Jazz # 5 – Jutta Hipp." 2011.

Donaldson, Bill. "An Interview with Jutta Hipp." *Marge Hofacre's Jazz News*, May/June,1998.

Feather, Leonard. "Jutta Hipp." *Jazz-Echo*, January, 1957.

Frank, Ryan. "Blazers, City Will Soon Discuss Developing Rose Quarter's Empty Lots." *The Oregonian*, June 24, 2010.

Grennard, Elliott. "Sparrow's Last Jump." *Harper's*, May, 1947.

Harrod, James. "The Lighthouse All Stars / June Christy." Stars of Jazz Blog, http://starsofjazz.blogspot.com, November 2, 2012.

Hatta, Masayuki, Matsubayashi, Kohji and Togashi, Nobuaki. "Stars Of Jazz Discography." The Jazz Discography Project, JAZZDISCO.org.

Hentoff, Nat. "Nouvelles d'Amérique. Hipp! Hipp! Hourrah!" *Jazz Hot*, March, 1956.

Hui Hsu, Judy Chia. "Jazz Great Eli Thompson Soared For 3 Decades, Fell Silent." *Seattle Times*, August 6, 2005.

Jazz-News. "Leonard Feather Awaits Jutta Hipp. " *Jazz-Echo*, July/August 1955.

Myers, Marc. "Buddy De Franco + Sonny Clark, Pt 2." *JazzWax*, January 29, 2010.

Myers, Marc. "Interview: Herb Geller." *JazzWax*, April 26, 2010.

Myers, Marc. "Jutta Hipp: The Inside Story." *JazzWax*, May 28, 2013.

Murakami, Haruki. "Three Short Essays on Jazz." *The Believer*, July/August, 2008.

The New Yorker. "Talk of the Town: Flipping." *The New Yorker*, March 31, 1956.

Ratliff, Ben. "Jutta Hipp, Jazz Pianist With a Percussive Style, Dies at 78." *The New York Times*, April 11, 2003.

Ratliff, Ben. "Lucky Thompson, Jazz Saxophonist, Is Dead at 81". *The New York Times*, August 5, 2005.

Reichman, Thomas. *Mingus: Charlie Mingus 1968*. 1968.

Sante, Luc. "I Thought I Heard Buddy Bolden Say." *The Believer*, November, 2004.

Showell, Jeffrey. "Jumptown: A Sad Legacy for Urban Renewal." *The Oregonian*, November 6, 2009.

Staff. "Jutta Hipp, 78; Traded Career as Jazz Pianist for a Job as Seamstress." *Los Angeles Times*, April 12, 2003.

Teddy Charles and the Westcoasters, *Adventures in California* CD.

Various authors: The original and reissue liner notes from Blue Note, Verve and Prestige albums, written by Michael Cuscuna, Ira Gitler, Bob Blumenthal, Nat Hentoff, Leonard Feather, Robert Levin, Ben Sidran, Joe Goldberg, Carl Woideck, Duke Pearson and Richard Seidel.

Von Schuttenbach, Katja. "Jutta Hipp: Talented and Unique Trail Blazer for Future Generations of Musicians." *Jazz Podium*, July/August, 2006.

Von Schuttenbach, Katja. Email interview, 2012.

Wardell Gray, *Wardell Gray Memorial, Vol. 1* CD.

About the author

Aaron Gilbreath is an essayist and journalist whose work has appeared in *Harper's*, *The New York Times*, *Paris Review*, *Vice*, *The Morning News*, *Saveur*, *Tin House*, *The Believer*, *Oxford American*, *Kenyon Review*, *Slate*, *Virginia Quarterly Review*, *The Threepenny Review*, and *Brick*. He is also the author of the essay collection *Everything We Don't Know* (Curbside Splendor, 2016).

CPSIA information can be obtained
at www.ICGtesting.com
Printed in the USA
FSOW01n1153100717
36233FS